AN INTRODUCTION

TO THE STUDY OF

ANGLO-MUHAMMADAN LAW

Owing to the antiquity and rarity of this book, certain pages are regrettably absent, and readability is compromised due to the blurring of the original text. If you possess any insights regarding the availability of these missing sections, kindly inform us. Your assistance is crucial in ensuring the completion of this significant work for the benefit of future generations.

AN INTRODUCTION

TO THE STUDY OF

ANGLO-MUHAMMADAN LAW

SIR ROLAND KNYVET WILSON

GYAN

Published by

GYAN

Gyan Publishing House
5, Ansari Road
Daryaganj, New Delhi-110002
Phone: 011-47034999, 9811692060
E-mail: books@gyanbooks.com

Distribution Network
gyanbooks.com
India, USA, Canada, UK, Australia

ISBN: 978-93-7169-451-3 (PB)

First Published, 1894

2nd Impression 2025

Printed at: Gyan Press, Delhi.

AN INTRODUCTION TO THE STUDY OF ANGLO-MUHAMMADAN LAW

Author: SIR ROLAND KNYVET WILSON

AN INTRODUCTION

TO THE STUDY OF

ANGLO-MUHAMMADAN LAW.

AN INTRODUCTION

TO THE STUDY OF

ANGLO-MUHAMMADAN LAW,

BY

SIR ROLAND KNYVET WILSON, BART., M.A., LL.M.,

BARRISTER-AT-LAW,

Late Reader in Indian Law to the University of Cambridge,

AUTHOR OF "MODERN ENGLISH LAW," ETC.

1894.

PREFACE.

FOURTEEN years' experience in the training of Selected Candidates for the Civil Service of India has impressed upon me that of all the branches of Indian Law which enter into their curriculum Muhammadan Law is the one in which there is most room for a new text-book. The chief existing deficiencies appear to me to be of two kinds. First, a lack of suitable introductory matter, to smooth the path of the beginner who approaches the subject with the ordinary intellectual outfit of English law-students; and secondly, insufficient recognition of the curiously composite character which the so-called Muhammadan Law of modern India has gradually come to assume under European manipulation. The present work aims primarily at supplying the first of these desiderata. The second receives some attention in the last two chapters; but for the precise and detailed information required by advanced students and practitioners I must ask my readers to wait for my forthcoming Digest of Anglo-Muhammadan Law, now in course of preparation.

The nature and extent of my obligations to previous writers, English, French, and German, may be gathered from the footnotes appended throughout. I make no pretension to Arabic scholarship, or any kind of original research, and shall be quite content if I am thought to have contributed appreciably to the better understanding of a somewhat neglected branch of legal study by appropriate selection and combination of fairly accessible but scattered materials.

CONTENTS.

ORTHOGRAPHY.

PROPER names and other Oriental words are spelt generally according to the system adopted by the Indian Government and by Dr. Hunter in the "Rulers of India" series. The vowels have the following sounds:—

a, as in wom*a*n (= *u* in f*u*n); *á*, as in f*a*ther; *e*, as in *e*gg; *i*, as in k*i*n; *í*, as in pol*i*ce; *o*, as in c*o*ld; *u*, as in b*u*ll; *ú*, as in r*u*le; *au*, as in German (= *ow* in f*ow*l).

But the popular spelling is preserved for a few very well-known names and titles, such as Mahomet (spelt Muhammad when it denotes any person other than the prophet), Caliph, etc.; and I have sometimes thought it unnecessary to encumber the page with accents where the phonetic difference would practically be unimportant.

LIST OF ABBREVIATIONS.

CULTURGESCH.—Culturgeschichte des Orients unter den Chalifen. Wien, 1875.

DIG.—The Digest, or Pandects, of Justinian.

HED.—Hedaya; pages as in Grady's abridgment of Hamilton's translation.

H.I.—Herrschenden Ideen des Islams, by Von Kremer. Leipzig, 1868.

K.—Korán.

SALE.—The 1892 edition of Sale's Korán, with preliminary discourse and notes; cited by the page, the verses not being numbered in this edition.

ANGLO-MUHAMMADAN LAW.

CHAPTER I.

MAHOMET AS A LEGISLATOR AND THE KORAN AS A LAW-BOOK.

" Every age hath its book ; God shall abolish and shall confirm what He pleaseth. With Him is the original of the Book."—*Koran*, chap. xiii.

What is Anglo-Muhammadan Law?

BRITISH rule in India has involved a succession of experiments in the proverbially difficult business of patching an old garment with new cloth; the old garment being the institutions and practices we call Oriental, the new cloth being rules of imperative law which in contradistinction to these we call European. Of these incongruous adjustments the most historically curious and the most practically important is the body of rules applied by the Civil Courts of India to the determination of certain kinds of disputes among so-called Hindús, constituting for this purpose, perhaps, half the total population of British India; but next in extent of application, and only a little inferior in importance, is the corresponding body of rules administered to the Muhammadan community, which numbers not much less than a fourth of the population.* The official designations of these two sets of rules are "Hindu Law" and "Muhammadan Law"; but inasmuch as each of these expressions signifies also to those whom it chiefly concerns an immense body of religious and ethical doctrine, accumulated in the course of ages round a nucleus of divine

* 49½ millions according to the census of 1891.

revelation, covering by its precepts the whole range of human action, and depending for its enforcement firstly on supernatural sanctions, secondly on various forms of social pressure, only thirdly and incidentally on the action of the law-courts—it seems better to distinguish by the prefix "Anglo" that small fragment of each system which an alien Government, making no pretence of sympathy with the general spirit of the whole, has thought suitable for enforcement by its own tribunals. British statesmanship determines from time to time how much of Oriental precept is to be treated as Law in the English sense, how much left to the consciences of those who acknowledge it as religiously binding, how much forcibly suppressed as noxious and immoral; and when this has been determined, European scholarship* sifts and classifies the Oriental authorities, the mental habits of English and Scotch lawyers* influence the methods of interpretation, and Procedure Codes of modern European manufacture regulate the ascertainment of the facts and the ultimate enforcement of the rule.

But if we wish to understand a compound phenomenon, it is well to begin by separately examining each factor in its uncompounded condition. I shall therefore first indicate the historic origin of European jurisprudence, and then trace the development of Muhammadan Law, in the primary and larger sense of that term, from its alleged supernatural origin to its contact with the Anglo-Indian variety of the former.

European and Oriental.

It is false history to connect the geographical epithets, "European" and "Oriental," with contrasted types of civilisation at any period earlier than the great wandering of the nations which overthrew, or transformed, the Roman Empire. The Greeks no doubt differed in important

---

* I mean to include under these expressions native scholars and native lawyers who follow European methods.

respects from their Eastern neighbours the Persians, but they differed quite as much from their Keltic neighbours to the North, and from the Carthaginians to the West; and when the Græco-Roman civilisation culminated, some of its richest provinces and brightest intellectual centres were to be found in Asia and Africa. The type of moral order which we now call European is indeed the product of that ancient civilisation as modified by acceptance of the Christian religion; but if we wish to find any common origin for the sentiments, practices, and forms of government which in contrast therewith we loosely call Oriental, we must look for it in the movement identified with the prophet of Arabia, and the geographical antithesis owes its only real significance to the fact that the Romanised and Christianised West withstood and ultimately rolled back the flood of Muhammadan conquest, which established a more permanent mastery in Central Asia and India. From the jurist's special point of view, the century from 534 to 634 A.D. constitutes the historic watershed, so to speak, on which the European and Oriental streams part company; and if I may venture to localise the metaphor by comparing the period in question to the Himalayan range, from which the Ganges and Brahmaputra flow off in opposite directions, then Anglo-Muhammadan Law is a part of the delta in which the mighty currents reluctantly approach each other and gradually commingle their waters, turbid with the deposits of widely distant regions, before finding their common goal in that all-embracing ocean of codified, cosmopolitan, simply rational jurisprudence which we believe to be somewhere between us and Utopia, but do not pretend to have surveyed.

Influence of Roman Law in the West.

The epoch of Justinian's legislation, 526-565 A.D., is perhaps the most important landmark in all legal history. To the European jurist its significance consists in this, that it compressed into a form capable of surviving through the dark ages some of the best work of a long extinct race of lawyers, produced under conditions not destined to recur for another thirteen centuries. Law allied with philosophy but divorced from one religion and not yet married to another,* backed by the power of the State but comparatively free from the intermeddling of mere politicians, having for its root the strongly-marked character of a single community, but shaped as it grew by influences ever more and more diversified, had been the favourite study of the keenest intellects during the first three centuries of Imperial Rome, and the results were not altogether unworthy of so remarkable a conjunction of favouring circumstances. In the civil branch of the law more especially, so much had been done to impart form and substance to men's intuitions of natural justice, so vast was the accumulation in the law libraries of hints for the solution of all probable controversies, and so easy were the legislative processes for the correction of anomalies, that if suitors failed to obtain justice, as it is to be feared they often did, the fault lay elsewhere than with the professional expositors of the law.

But already, nearly three centuries before Justinian, the golden age of Roman jurisprudence had come to an end. Ulpian and Modestinus left no successors capable of taking up the chief task still remaining to be accomplished, that of sifting and condensing the materials already

---

* I reckon this as an advantage for the purpose in hand, not as denying that legislative or any other business is the better for being performed in a religious spirit, but because, historically, the claim of a specific Divine origin for a set of human rules has usually been made in a shape extremely adverse to criticism and amendment. And while I echo here the common opinion as to the essentially secular character of the work of the Antonine jurists, I must confess to some doubt as to whether it is, after all, anything more than the expression of our ignorance, considering how small a proportion of the whole has been preserved to us, and that by compilers who would naturally omit everything distinctively Pagan. See Addis, "Christianity and the Roman Empire," chap. i.

accumulated. The best intellect of the age had begun to find its employment in theology, and from the conversion of Constantine the maintenance, reform, or abolition of the civil laws of Rome depended on the attitude of the Christian Church. The experience of two more centuries sufficed to make it clear that the new religion had no particular legal system of its own, and would be content to build on the old foundations. Whether it were attributed to the feeble following and premature death of the Founder of Christianity, or to a deliberate conviction on his part that force could under no circumstances be a suitable remedy for human wrongs, the fact was unquestionable that no recorded word or act of his threw any light whatever on the proper mode of exercising political power, or on the principles of legislation. But to whatever extent the Christians before Constantine may have followed the advice of St. Paul to appoint arbitrators among themselves for the settlement of secular disputes, there is no reason to suppose that such arbitrators would as a rule look for guidance to any other source than the contemporary Roman Law, or that the bishops, who after Constantine were invested with regular civil jurisdiction, would hesitate to consult the ordinary law libraries in cases involving no question of Paganism or heresy.

The way having been thus cleared for a revival of the study of jurisprudence, and the point having been reached at which condensation rather than further discussion was the chief thing needful, we come after certain less successful experiments to the famous Corpus Juris of Justinian, of which the most permanently useful portions were a collection of extracts from the writings of the classical jurists, published under the name of "The Digests, or Pandects," and a modernised version of the lecture notes of an ancient pagan law professor,* known thenceforth as the Institutes of

* Gaius, about 150 A.D.

Justinian. The fact of this same Emperor just about that time adding Italy to his dominions, and also the fact of his posing as a champion of Christian orthodoxy, facilitated the reception of this body of law among the nations which afterwards made up Latin Christendom. And thus it has come to pass that, in spite of the great part played in European history by organised priesthoods, all European systems of law, including the English, rest, broadly speaking, on a secular basis, not built up by ingenious commentators on a foundation of infallible Scripture, but by Governments freely legislating to meet the needs of their own time; influenced by the example, yet not overpowered by the authority, of the cosmopolitan, unsacerdotal jurists of the Antonine era.

Fate of Justinian's Legislation in the East.

It may be doubted whether Justinian's immediate subjects derived any very great benefit from the Corpus Juris. Most of it was in Latin, whereas the bulk of them spoke Greek, and some Syriac or Arabic. It was repeatedly and capriciously altered by the legislator himself during the last thirty years of his reign. And there are other reasons for supposing that the Imperial enactments of this period seldom made themselves felt much beyond the chief centres of administration, and that in the outlying districts of the Eastern provinces the regular tribunals were less resorted to than clerical arbitrators, the bishops and presbyters of the different sects, whose legal notions were derived at second or third hand from the older Roman law sources,* with an admixture of other elements.

In short, the prevailing tendency to distrust natural reason

---

* German research has brought to light just such a book as these arbitrators would be likely to use; composed in Greek, apparently by an ecclesiastic, some fifty years before Justinian's time; translated successively into Syriac, Armenian, and Arabic; and shown to have been current from Armenia to Egypt inclusive far down into the Middle Ages. Syrisch-Römisches Rechtsbuch, ed. Bruns and Sachau.

as a guide to legislation, to prefer priests to lawyers as dispensers of justice, and to render but cold and perfunctory obedience to laws unprovided with supernatural credentials, was checked in the West by the immense prestige, coupled with the confessedly non-Christian origin, of the Pandects and the Institutes. In the Eastern provinces the weight of this counterpoise was greatly attenuated, while at the same time the essentially non-legal character of Christianity gave a certain air of unreality to all attempts to make the decisions of clerical tribunals seem like the decrees of heaven, and this want of harmony between religion and law may help to explain the temporary triumph of a rival system at once frankly militant and uncompromisingly theocratic.

Rudiments of Law in Pre-Islamite Arabia.

Can we speak of the countrymen of Mahomet as having been governed by law in any and what sense at the time when he commenced his mission?

That they were not governed by Roman law goes without saying, unless indeed we are to reckon among the prophet's countrymen those tribes of Arab descent who were settled within the limits of the Empire. Some Christian Arabs formed a kingdom tributary to Constantinople stretching along the North-west frontier; but that they were in any other sense Romanised, even to the extent of using the Syro-Roman law-book, there is nothing to show, any more than that the Arabs who occupied the corresponding strip along the Persian frontier and paid tribute to that Empire were in any other respect Persianised. The most civilised part of Arabia was the kingdom of Yemen in the South, which was transferred about this time from the Jews to the Christian Abyssinians and from these again to the Persians.

Over the immense intervening expanse nothing deserving the name of "habitual obedience to a common superior" was rendered by any assemblage of persons larger than a petty tribe. And if there was little government there was still less law; in other words, where habits of obedience existed, they were habits of obeying such occasional commands as the exigencies of a foray or an internal squabble might evoke, and for any chief or council solemnly to enunciate general rules of conduct for the future guidance of the community would have seemed the merest pedantry and presumption.*

The absence of law and government properly so called does not exclude all agencies for the repression of individual or tribal aggressiveness. There may yet remain the force of religion, the force of public opinion, the instinctive preference which some have for tranquillity as others have for strife. It is true, however, that according to general experience all these social agencies have a strong tendency to transmute themselves into powerful governments and regular tribunals as soon as they have attained a certain measure of intensity, so that the absence of political and legal organisation is presumptive, though not conclusive, evidence of a low level of moral sentiment, and it was so among the Arabs. Their religion had just enough of the social element in it to draw crowds together for the worship of some favourite object, such as the black stone in the Kaaba at Mecca, especially when the place happened to be also a convenient commercial entrepôt, and to bring about some sort of understanding that the normal state of intertribal warfare should be suspended during the two months set apart for these gatherings; and these same meetings supplied some slight amount of force and concentration to intertribal public opinion, at the cost of reviving old feuds and provoking new ones, owing to the custom of reciting poems, often of a satirical character. Lastly, the custom of the bloodfeud, *i.e.*, that the death of a tribesman should be avenged at all costs by the death of some mem-

* See Muir's "Life of Mahomet," Introd. p. vi.

ber, no matter which, of the offender's tribe, could scarcely have had more binding force had it been in very truth a law, so deeply-rooted was it in the general sentiment. Whatever amount of external protection this custom may have afforded, it had no tendency to shield the women and children of a family against the male adults; the impulses of natural affection were too often unequally matched against the suggestions of avarice, lust, superstition, and false pride; and thus we find among the usages revealed to us through their subsequent condemnation, the plundering of male orphans by their brothers, uncles or cousins, the general denial of rights of inheritance (if not of all rights of property*) to females; the enforced marriage of female orphans to their nearest male relative other than a brother, and of widows to the father, son, or brother of the deceased husband, or as an alternative their sale to a strange suitor; the sale of daughters in marriage, or in families where this had come to be thought disgraceful, the burying alive of infant daughters in order to avoid the burden of maintaining them and the trouble of finding a suitable husband. Marriage itself, in any sense implying even one-sided conjugal fidelity and consequent ascertainment of paternity, is said† to have been a modern improvement, dating from only a century or so before Mahomet. Even affection for male offspring was not proof against the suggestions of a cruel superstition, and Mahomet's own father narrowly escaped being sacrificed by his father in fulfilment of a rash vow. In short, it is much easier to multiply instances of objectionable practices on which Pre-Islamite usage imposed no check, than to find an example

* As to the exceptional cases in which women do seem to have held property, see Robertson Smith, "Kinship and Marriage in Early Arabia." Chap. iii.

† By Professor Robertson Smith, "Kinship and Marriage in Early Arabia," pp. 69, 107.

of really restrictive custom having anything approaching to the force of law.

Mahomet as Prophet and Ruler.

It is quite in accordance with the genius of Islam that the event which determines the commencement of the Muhammadan era is not the birth of the prophet, nor the first announcement of his divine mission, but his first assumption of political and military authority. To us, who are only concerned with the religion in so far as it is the basis of a system of civil law, the appropriateness of this era is still more unquestionable. Before the Hijra,* or "Flight" (A.D. 622), the foundation of Mahomet's spiritual ascendancy had been laid by eleven years of incessant preaching in the market-place of Mecca; but, though his utterances of that period as recorded in the Korân are more impressive as compositions than those of later date, the jurist has nothing to do with the denunciations of idolatry, descriptions of heaven and hell, assertions of his own divine commission and comparisons of himself to the prophets his predecessors, which make up nearly the whole of their contents.

"I am only a warner, I have no authority over you," was his habitual language at Mecca.† It was in truth the only tone he could without absurdity adopt while he was dependent for his very life on the protection of an unconverted uncle, and had to look on helplessly at the martyrdom or flight of his less powerfully befriended disciples. What is strikingly illustrated by this stage in his career is the strength, and also the weakness, of the vendetta system as a substitute for law and police. The attacks levelled at the

* Pronounced "Hidgerah." The old-fashioned spelling was apt to mislead the unwary into talking of the Hegīra. Muhammadan writers usually date events according to the number of *lunar* years from the Hijra. In order to convert A.H. into A.D., deduct three per cent. from the former, and then add 622 to the remainder.

† See K. xlvi. 7., lxxxviii. 10.

most cherished beliefs and institutions of his countrymen were such as would have led to his trial and punishment in almost any State, ancient or modern, and did in fact excite deadly hatred in the breasts of those who formed the nearest approach to a governing body that the city possessed; yet he and those of his adherents who had kinsmen bound by custom to avenge them remained personally unharmed for several years, while those who had not were tortured or killed at the pleasure of this or that individual.

The flight from Mecca to Yathrib, thenceforth called Medina, entirely altered his position. Before accepting the invitation of his partisans in that city, he had received from them a solemn promise to obey him in all things lawful and to defend him as they would defend their own wives and children. Those who fled with him were already bound to at least equally strict obedience, and gradually all the Arab inhabitants of Medina were either persuaded or compelled to acknowledge his authority. The three Jewish tribes in the neighbourhood were at first disposed to welcome him as the champion of monotheism, but were bitterly disappointed when he held up Jesus as the last and greatest of the prophets except himself, still more when he decided for Mecca instead of Jerusalem as the centre of the new worship; they displayed their hostility whenever they dared, and were at last either massacred or expelled. Thenceforth his power was practically absolute in Medina. "I have seen," reported the deputy from Mecca, "the Chosroes of Persia and the Cæsar of Rome,* but never did I behold a king among his subjects like Mahomet among his companions." His political functions, however, were exercised through the prophetic office. The mosque was his council chamber and hall of audience; the Friday sermon was his chief opportunity for declarations of

* Constantinople, officially designated as "New Rome," and generally known in the East as "Roum."

policy, and in any matter requiring any special deliberation it was his wont to wait till the usual symptoms of inspiration came upon him, and he could announce a special message from heaven bearing directly on the point. Naturally such messages, delivered as from God to himself in the second person, referred more pointedly to divine than to human punishments in case of disobedience, but the latter were not wanting on occasion. Before his supremacy was completely established, these sometimes took the form of swift and secret assassinations, publicly avowed and gloried in after their accomplishment; but an example of true criminal jurisdiction, openly though very informally exercised, is supplied by the case of Hârith, who at the disastrous battle of Ohod took advantage of the confusion to slay a fellow Moslem in prosecution of a family vendetta. The sequel is thus related by Sir William Muir ("Life of Mahomet," p. 281.)

"A comrade, who was witness to the deed, reported it to Mahomet. An investigation was held, and the crime brought home to Hârith*. Shortly after his return from Hamru ul Asád, the prophet called for his ass, and rode forth to Coba. It was not one of the days (Saturday and Monday) on which he ordinarily repaired to that suburb, and the men of Upper Medina boded no good from his unusual visit. He entered the mosque and received the salutation of the chief inhabitants of the vicinity. At length the culprit himself, clothed in a yellow dress, and little anticipating the event, came up. Perceiving him approach, Mahomet called aloud to Oweim, a chief of the Bani Aus: "Take Hârith, the son of Suweid, unto the gate of the mosque, and there strike off his head, because of Mujaddzir, the son of Dziad, for verily he slew him on the day of Ohod." Oweim prepared to obey the

* The context implies that Hârith had no notice of the accusation until he heard the order for his execution; but, as he then urged nothing in his defence, substantial justice was probably done.

command, when Hârith desired leave to speak, and hastening towards Mahomet, laid hold of his stirrup as he was about to mount his ass. He begged for mercy, and promised to expiate the crime by any sacrifice the Prophet might direct. Mahomet turned from him, and reiterated the order for his execution. Seeing the decree to be irrevocable, Oweim dragged Hârith back to the gate, and there beheaded him, in the presence of Mahomet, the sons of Mujaddzir, and the assembled chiefs. The assumption of supreme authority was unquestioned, and it is indicative of the absolute command now exercised by the prophet over the whole city."

Another story, told by the same historian, well illustrates Mahomet's exercise of civil jurisdiction.

"Among the slain (at the battle of Ohod) was Sád, the son of Rabi, a leader of the Bani Khazraj. He left a widow and two daughters; but his brother, according to the practice of the times, took possession of the whole inheritance. The widow was grieved at this, and being a discreet and prudent person, pondered how she might obtain redress. She invited Mahomet to a feast, with about twenty of his chief companions. He agreed to go. A retired spot among the palm trees of her garden was well sprinkled with water, and the repast spread. Mahomet arrived, and with his followers seated himself upon the carpets prepared for them. He spoke kindly to the widow of her husband's memory, so that all the women wept, and the eyes of the prophet also filled with tears. The supper was then eaten, and a feast of fresh dates followed. When the repast was over, the widow arose, and thus disclosed her grief:—"Sád, as thou well knowest, was slain at Ohod. His brother hath seized the inheritance. There is nothing left for the two daughters; and how shall they be married without a portion?" Mahomet, moved by the simple tale, replied:—"The Lord shall decide regarding the inheritance, for no command hath yet been revealed to me in this matter. Come again unto me when I shall have returned home." So he departed. Shortly afterwards, as he sat with his companions at the door of his own house symptoms of inspiration came upon him ; he was oppressed, and the drops of sweat fell like pearls from his forehead. Then he commanded that the widow of Sád and his brother should be summoned. When they were brought before him, he thus addressed the brother :—"Restore unto the daughters of Sád two-thirds of that which he hath left behind, and one-eighth part unto his widow ; the remainder is for thee." The widow was overjoyed, and uttered the Takbír, "Great is the Lord !" Such is the origin of one of the main provisions of the Muhammadan law of inheritance."*

The concluding sentence of the above extract suggests the question, Granting that Mahomet governed, judged, and punished, just like a temporal sovereign, did he also *legislate ?*

Mahomet as Legislator.

To satisfy the modern definition of a legislative enactment three elements must concur: generality, penality, and political sovereignty as the source of the latter. A permanent rule of conduct must be enunciated, an *intention* to punish infractions of the rule (not a mere *expectation* that unpleasant consequences will ensue) must be intimated, and the threat must purport to be backed by the collective force of the community, concentrated in the hands of some human person or assembly.

Now at Mecca, before the Flight, Mahomet was constantly enunciating general rules of conduct, and was also constantly painting the most horrible pictures of what he expected to happen, in this world or the next, as the result of disobedience ; but he wielded no political power, and spoke only as a "warner." At Medina he possessed political power, but the struggle to maintain and extend it absorbed so large a part of his energies as to leave but little leisure for systema-

* Muir's "Life of Mahomet."

tising. Moreover, being prophet as well as sovereign, and only sovereign because prophet, he reserved his most deliberate and comprehensive injunctions for the solemn occasions on which he spoke as the very mouthpiece of the Deity. In that capacity he naturally dwelt chiefly on divine rewards and punishments, and was not very careful to distinguish counsels of perfection addressed to the conscience from rules to be enforced by judicial officers.

There was the less need for discrimination because, until a year or two before his death, the concern was not too large to admit of his being consulted promptly and personally in every difficulty. After the conquest of Mecca, and the consequent submission of the greater part of Arabia, it did become necessary to send out commissioners far beyond the range of daily communication with head-quarters, and therefore to furnish them with general instructions as to how they were to deal with the new converts—what was to be obligatory and what optional.* If we had these instructions in full, we should, perhaps, gather from them Mahomet's ripest notions of legislative method; but, as it is, we must find what we are in search of in the Korán or nowhere.

The Korán as a Law-book.

Confining our attention, for the reason already given, to the Suras† delivered (certainly or possibly) at Medina, we find their number to be at most twenty-seven out of a total of 114, making up in actual bulk between a third and a fourth of the whole. Even of these, most are entirely, and all chiefly, occupied with non-legal matter, hortatory, theological, or merely personal; but it is possible to cull from different chapters some eighty or ninety verses, constituting about

* Muir's "Life of Mahomet," p. 476.

† *I.e*, chapters. The word is said to signify a course of bricks in a wall, hence any continuous portion of a work complete in itself. See Palmer's "Koran," p. lvi. Introd.

$\frac{1}{50}$th of the entire Korán, which lay down something like a general rule on matters which might come before a civil or criminal court of justice. Even these are very largely open to the observation that the sanction put in the foreground is the religious one. The passages which convey a distinct intimation that it is the duty of Moslems to visit offenders against the rule in question with temporal penalties are very few indeed. Such are the two texts in Chap. v., prescribing the punishments for treason and theft respectively; but even of these the former is so worded as to represent the prescribed punishment as merely a foretaste of hell fire. Another famous rule, viz., that in Chap. ii. against usury, begins by saying that "those who devour usury shall not rise again, save as he riseth whom Satan hath paralysed with a touch," and that "God shall blot out usury, but shall make almsgiving profitable;" but it goes on to say, "O ye who believe, fear God and remit the balance of usury, if ye be believers; *and if ye will not do it, then hearken to the proclamation of war from God and His Apostle; but if ye repent, your capital is yours.*"

In most cases we can only infer with more or less probability, from the nature of each particular injunction, whether or not it was intended by Mahomet to be in a secular sense imperative.

For instance, the fourth Sura opens with general exhortations to fear God, and then proceeds to inculcate the duty of justice and kindness to orphan relatives, dovetailing somewhat oddly into the middle of this topic the famous passage which is supposed to establish both the legality and the limitations of polygamy, and then clenching the matter with arguments addressed to the conscience of the hearer and to his fear of the divine judgments. "And let these fear lest they leave behind them a weak seed for whom they would be afraid; and let them fear God, and speak a straightforward speech. Verily, those who devour the property of orphans unjustly, only devour into their bellies fire, and they shall broil in flames." Then come the well-known texts which constitute to this day the backbone of the Law of Inheritance, and which generalise (among other things) the effect of the above-mentioned decision in favour of the widow and daughters of Sád. This passage also concludes with references to paradise and hell-fire. But we feel pretty well assured, as we read the story of the Sád succession case, that if the brother had attempted to retain possession in defiance of the decree he would by no means have been left undisturbed till the Day of Judgment; nor is it any more conceivable that a dishonest guardian would have been allowed to waste his ward's property so long as he was prepared to take his chance of broiling in flames hereafter.

On the other hand, the recommendations in the second Sura to put contracts in writing for the prevention of disputes leave us in doubt whether they are mere advice, or whether the neglect of the prescribed formalities, like failure to satisfy the requirements of the English Statute of Frauds, was meant to be an absolute bar to any action on the contract. And such general directions as that of K. lxiii. 10, to "expend in alms of what we have bestowed upon you before death cometh upon any one of you," are manifestly only moral exhortations, though quoted by Muhammadan doctors as though they were of themselves sufficient to establish that definite obligation to pay tithe, which we happen to know from other sources to have been, in fact, enforced by Mahomet as well as by his successors.*

Increased Importance of the Korán after the Death of Mahomet.

It really mattered little to the Arabs how much of the Korán was of general and permanent, and how much of merely individual and temporary application, so long as the channel of fresh inspiration was kept open, and the current

* See, for instance, the Hedaya, Book I. Chap. I., Grady's edition, p. 1.

was running freely. Obedience to God and obedience to His Apostle were never separated even in thought, and experience had led them confidently to expect that for each new emergency a new verse or chapter of the Korán would be "sent down," possibly even abrogating a previous revelation, "Whatever verse we annul, or cause thee to forget, we will bring a better one than it, or one like unto it."*

Probably not one of them had analysed his own motives sufficiently to say whether he rendered allegiance to the Prophet because he approved of his principles, or interested himself in the principles because of his admiration for the man, until the critical moment (A.D. 632) when Abu Bakr came forth from the chamber of death and said to the assembly, "Let him know, whosoever worshippeth Mahomet, that Mahomet indeed is dead; but whoso worshippeth God, let him know that the Lord liveth, and doth not die."†

In the spirit of that declaration, after a short period of indecision and confusion, Abu Bakr himself, the Prophet's oldest friend and the father of his favourite wife, was chosen to carry on the work as Caliph (Khalifa) *i.e.*, successor. But on the question, what exactly was the work to be carried on, perhaps the only points quite clear to every one were that it included the prosecution of the wars already on foot against the Byzantine Empire, and against certain rival prophets in Arabia, and the maintenance of a common government for all who had once tendered allegiance to the prophet. The watchword was still "Obedience to God and His Apostle;" but the latter part of the formula evidently required fresh explanation. The words of Omar, in recanting his first passionate assertion that Mahomet was not dead, and could not die, and in proposing the election of Abu Bakr, intimate plainly

* K. II. 100. † Muir's "Caliphate," p. 2, ed. 1891.

enough the only sense in which allegiance to a dead prophet could still be inculcated.

"O ye people, that which I spoke unto you yesterday was not the truth. Verily I find that it is not borne out by the Book which the Lord hath revealed,* nor by the covenant which we made with His Apostle. As for me, verily I hoped that the Apostle of the Lord would continue yet awhile amongst us, and speak in our ears a word such as might seem good to him, and be a perpetual guide unto us. But the Lord hath chosen for His Apostle the portion which is with Himself in preference to the portion which is with you. And truly, the inspired word which directed your Prophet is with us still. Take it, therefore, for your guide, and ye shall never go astray."

The speech of Abu Bakr in acknowledging his election, does not repeat the reference to the Book, but dwells on the two points of even-handed justice, and "fighting in the ways of the Lord," as though these were the essence of the faith of Islam.

"Ye people! now, verily, I have become the chief over you, though I am not the best amongst you. If I do well, support me; if I err, then set me right. In truth and in sincerity is faithfulness, and in falsehood, perfidy. The weak and oppressed in my sight shall be strong, until I restore his right to him, if the Lord will; and the strong oppressor among you shall be weak, until I wrest from him that which he hath usurped. Now, hearken to me: When a people leaveth off to fight in the ways of the Lord, verily He casteth them away in disgrace. Know, also, that wickedness never abounded in any nation but the Lord visited that nation with calamity. Wherefore, obey me, even as I shall obey the Lord and His

* The reference is to K. iii. 136. "Mahomet is no more than an Apostle; other apostles have already deceased before him; if he die therefore, or be slain, will ye therefore turn back on your heels?"

Apostle. Whensoever I disobey them, obedience is no longer obligatory upon you. Arise to prayers, and the Lord have mercy upon you!"

The "Book," referred to in the first of these speeches, had, as yet, no material existence as such—at least, on this earth. It was believed, on the authority of Mahomet—as we gather partly from the Korán itself, and partly from tradition—that a great volume, or "preserved table," of the Divine decrees, had lain before the throne of God from all eternity; that a copy of this was brought down by the angel Gabriel on the "night of power" to the lowest heaven, from whence the angel brought portions to Mahomet, and dictated them to him as occasion required. He wrote nothing down, being, in fact, unable to write according to his own account, but learnt it by heart, and recited it to an audience which was, for the most part, equally illiterate.* Occasionally, the few disciples who were capable of doing so would write down particular portions for their own use, which they would retain in their own custody; but, for the most part, reliance was placed, both during the Prophet's lifetime, and for a year or so after his death, on a class of "Korán Readers" (more properly, reciters), who strained naturally retentive memories to the utmost while vying with each other who should repeat the longest portions by heart.

The insecurity of this resource was forcibly brought home to the Caliph and his advisers by the bloody battle of Yemáma (633 A.D.), in which a large number of these "Readers" were slain; and scattered scraps of private manuscript were, of course, wholly inadequate to meet a

* Ameer Ali ("Spirit of Islam," p. 533) thinks that the nucleus of an educational institution was formed at Medina in the Prophet's lifetime; but if so, it must have been extremely rudimentary. Gobineau ("Les Religions et les Philosophies dans l'Asie Centrale," p. 49) is convinced from internal evidence that the Korán is the work, not merely of a person able to read and write, but of a person profoundly acquainted with the peculiar learning which he calls Aramean, and with the corresponding highly artificial forms of expression.

great public want. The logic of the situation imperatively required a complete and properly authenticated record of the series of divine messages, now closed for ever, obedience to which was to be enforced at the sword's point. So a commission was given to one Zeíd, the son of Thábit, who had acted as amanuensis to the Prophet, to "search out the Korán, and bring it together"; and the result, as gathered from "palm-leaves, skins, blade-bones, and the hearts of men," is generally allowed to have been very nearly identical with the present text.

Once, and only once, has it been authoritatively revised since that time; namely, in the reign of Othman, the third caliph, about 651 A.D., and this measure seems to have been suggested, not by any doubt as to the substantial accuracy of the original, which had remained all the time in the custody of Hafsa, daughter of Omar and widow of the Prophet, but partly by the need for more accurate indications as to the manner in which it was to be read, partly by the multiplication of inaccurate copies in the widely-distant regions over which the faithful were now dispersed. The original editor was a member of the revising committee, his coadjutors being three individuals of the tribe of Koreish, supposed to be better authorities for the dialect of Mecca. They did not even venture to remedy the most glaring defect of the first edition, namely, the absence of any principle of arrangement, logical or chronological. Sir William Muir assures us that the text of Othman's recension has been so carefully preserved that "there are no variations of importance—we may almost say no variations at all—among the innumerable copies of the Korán scattered throughout the vast bounds of the Empire of Islám."*

Conclusion.

Such, then, is the original and fundamental code of Islám; and thus, exactly a century after the publication of the code

* Sir William Muir's "Life of Mahomet," Excursus, on "The Sources," and "Caliphate," p. 218. See note at end of the chapter.

which closes the history of Roman law as a national system, we arrive at the beginning of law, properly so-called, in a neighbouring but singularly unconnected community. With the code nearest to it in point of time it has no connection or analogy; with the code with which Roman legal history is sometimes said to commence there are some notable points of resemblance, though more of contrast.

Like the enactment of the Twelve Tables, the promulgation of the Korán by Abu Bakr was substantially the act of an organised political society, imposing rules of conduct upon each and all of its members, to be enforced in case of need by its collective physical force. Like that code, only more literally and absolutely, it was the beginning of legal history for the people to whom it was addressed. In both cases the community originally legislated for was small, homogeneous, and unsophisticated, but grew into a vast cosmopolitan aggregate, with wholly different and far more complicated requirements.

But, unlike the Decemviral code, which was compiled in a business-like way for the guidance of magistrates and litigants, and which made no pretence of finality, the Korán is, as we have seen, *a religious miscellany with some legislative matter embedded in it*, which would never have been put forward to do duty as a code but for the belief, common to rulers and ruled, that every word and every syllable came direct from heaven; and which having been put forward in that belief, cannot be abrogated or altered in the smallest particular until a new divine messenger shall present himself with equally good credentials.

Note.—Since these pages were printed, I have seen it stated in the *Times* that the original of Othman's edition, carefully preserved in the chief mosque at Damascus, was destroyed in the great fire of October, 1893.

CHAPTER II.

The Post-Koranic Development of Muhammadan Law, so far as it proceeded on Orthodox Lines.

The Arabs are the only people of the early Middle Ages who, in respect of the development and scientific elaboration of the idea of Law, can show results at all approaching in grandeur to the creations of the Romans, those legislators for the world. Von Kremer, "Culturgeschichte des Orients," Vol. I., p. 470.

The "Rightly-directed" Caliphs.

The embarrassments foreshadowed at the close of the preceding chapter, as likely to result from the adoption of such a work as the Korán as the unalterable basis of a system of civil law, did not immediately make themselves felt. During the ten years' struggle which established the Prophet's ascendancy, his methods of governing and administering justice must have been the chief topic of conversation throughout the length and breadth of Arabia, and must have become familiar in a general way to every Arab old enough and intelligent enough to take any interest in public affairs; while an exhaustive knowledge of all that Mahomet had done, or said, or even thought, coupled with the most single-minded desire to tread as closely as possible in his footsteps, might reasonably be presumed from the antecedents of the first two Caliphs, Abu Bakr and Omar. And although the factions which rent the State under the third and fourth Caliphs prove that neither of them enjoyed to the same extent the general confidence of the faithful in their capacity of rulers, still, *as interpreters of the mind of the departed founder*, the qualifications of his two sons-in-law,

Othman and Ali, were very little, if at all, inferior to those of their predecessors. At all events they were surrounded by too many of the surviving companions, the heroes of Bedr and Ohod, to go far astray in matters of ritual or dogma, or in the determination of private disputes, and thus all four came to be classed together in orthodox tradition as the "rightly-directed Caliphs,"* or, as the phrase is often varied, the Imáms. The title Imám denotes spiritual leadership, and implies the right to conduct public worship, and to decide questions of conscience and law. In Moslem theory the Caliph is necessarily also supreme Imám; but the circumstances now to be described tended to make the latter title less and less appropriate to the possessor of executive power.

The Omayad Dynasty.

But a widely different state of things presents itself after the death of Ali, coinciding as it does with the general dying out of the generation of the Prophet's contemporaries. The seat of government had been removed from Medina to Damascus, and its sway had come to extend over regions only vaguely known to the Prophet, over millions of Greek and Persian converts, and perhaps still more numerous unconverted tributaries, accustomed to institutions differing widely from those which the Korán presupposed. The new ruler was the son of Mahomet's leading opponent, and though he had himself been taken into favour and even confidentially employed during the last year of the Prophet's life, it was not for that reason that the Moslems obeyed him, but simply because a combination of good fortune, energy, and worldly wisdom seemed to point him out as the best

---

* Abu Bakr,	632-634 A.D.
Omar,	634-644 A.D.
Othman,	644-655 A.D.
Ali.	655-661 A.D.

available guardian of the material interests of the empire. This was quite enough to account for his supremacy, but it was not enough to justify it in the eyes of devout Moslems, or to prove that in obeying him they were obeying God and His Apostle. Still less could they feel any such confidence under Muáwia's successors, several of whom were notorious violators of some of the plainest precepts of the Korán, and on whom lay the odium of a cruel massacre of the Prophet's family and of the sack of the two Holy Cities.*

Demand for more Divine Law.

The ordinances of these Omayad Caliphs were no doubt laws in the modern Austinian sense† so far as their sovereignty extended; in other words, so far as each could be said to be habitually obeyed by the bulk of the Moslem community; but that was not saying very much. From the death of Muáwia (A.D. 680), to the final collapse of the dynasty (A.D. 750), very few years passed without a rebellion somewhere, and there is not much rashness in surmising that at least one main cause of this precariousness of obedience was the general conviction that the commands of human rulers ought only to be obeyed so far as in accordance with the Divine Law, coupled with the greatest uncertainty as to what the Divine Law really enjoined on many points of constant occurrence, from the principles which should govern the succession to the Caliphate to the question whether the worshippers' nose must be rubbed in the dust at each prostration. An increase in the quantity of fixed Divine Law appeared eminently desirable to both rulers and subjects, though for different reasons; to the subjects, because bitter experience taught them the hopelessness of looking for any more "rightly-directed" Caliphs, and the next best thing was to find rules which could

---

* As to this, see the next chapter. † As to this, see Appendix.

command some degree of respect under good and bad princes alike; to the rulers, because even the worst sovereign finds his security promoted by his subordinates observing fixed rules in the ninety-nine cases which do not touch his personal interests, and the master of legions may reasonably hope to find some means of preventing their too stringent application to himself in the 100th case in which they might incommode him.

Growth of a Class of Jurists.

This strong and continuous demand gradually elicited a supply of professional expositors of the Shariat, or Sacred Law, as it ultimately came to be called, somewhat analogous to the class of *jurisprudentes* among the Romans. Indeed, it is not unlikely that the resemblance may have been in some degree the result of direct imitation. For, at the time when the provinces of Syria and Egypt were torn from the Byzantine Empire, regular schools for the study of Roman law were still in existence at Berytus and Alexandria, and though the Moslems were precluded by their principles from displaying any special interest either in the writings of Pagan jurists* or in enactments of Christian Emperors, yet they could hardly help becoming acquainted with the fashion in which their Christian subjects set about ascertaining a point of law; and, what is even more important, they could have no experience or conception of any other mode, Pre-Islamite Arabia having had, as we have seen, too little law to maintain a class of lawyers, and the ten years' personal rule of Mahomet having simply accustomed the Arabs to look for a solution to be telegraphed direct from heaven for each legal difficulty as it arose. And now, look where they might among the majestic ruins of that ancient civilisation which they were trampling under foot but aspired to replace,

* The law professors themselves of this period and of those provinces would perhaps know the contents of Justinian's "Digest" only through Greek translations or epitomes.

substantially only two methods of law-making would disclose themselves: the method of direct legislation, and what I may call the jurisprudential method.

According to this latter, students, clients, and magistrates alike consult those whom they think most competent to give opinions on cases about which they happen to feel a doubt, whether such cases be purely hypothetical, or cases on which litigation is contemplated, or cases actually awaiting the decision of the magistrate, who will not trust himself to give it without the guidance of the jurisconsult. These opinions (*responsa*) carry weight in proportion to the reputation of their authors, and the weightiest of them being collected into standard text-books, to be in turn made the subject of commentaries which will ultimately be condensed into digests, attain at some stage, it is difficult to say exactly when, an authority which no magistrate will venture to dispute, and thus become an integral part of the positive law of the community.

A third method of law-making now divides with direct legislation the favour of modern English-speaking communities, which combines in the same person the functions of judge, jurisconsult and legislator, and accepts as law for the future the principle assumed by the judge as the ground of decision in a concrete case actually litigated; but this case-law, or judiciary law, is barely to be discerned in embryo on a close analysis of the Imperial Constitutions, and practically did not exist in any form which could attract the attention of the Arabs.

Direct statutory legislation being inadmissible for the reasons already indicated, jurisprudential law-making was for most purposes the only available method, and thus we find, as the Moslem counterpart to the *jurisprudens* or *jurisconsultus*, the Maulawi,* or Mufti; the former term denoting that he is a professor of *the* science *par excellence*,

---

* Also written Moulvi, or Moollah.

the knowledge of the Divine Law,* the latter that his function is to give responses (*fatwas*) either to private individuals consulting him on questions of conscience or of law, or to the magistrate (*kázi*), or to the Caliph himself, on questions of law. The *maulawi* may happen to hold a judicial appointment as *kázi;* but it is his opinion as *maulawi*, not his decree as *kázi*, which (if anything) is recorded for future guidance, and contributes to the development of the *Shariat.*

The whole body of persons devoted to the pursuit of sacred learning is known collectively as the *ulama*, a word derived from the same root as *maulawi;* and it is the general opinion of this body, † not that of the executive head of the State, which determines who among its past and present members are entitled to be regarded as standard authorities (*mujtahids*). No doubt the Caliphs of the Omayad and Abbasside dynasties could, and did to a certain extent, influence the current of legal decisions through the exercise of patronage in the shape of judgeships and endowed professorships, but they interfered on the whole far less than the Roman Emperors, and were less closely in touch with the leading jurists of their time. As to their nominal power of deciding questions of law on their own account in their capacity of Imám, its exercise became practically impossible when once the Sacred Law was admitted to be an intricate science, demanding the study of a lifetime. They might, no doubt, have imitated the Roman Emperors by endorsing *pro forma* decisions drafted by their legal advisers, but apparently they never did. And the Sultans who ultimately superseded the Caliphs did not, I think, even pretend

* Compare Ulpian; jurisprudentia est divinarum atque humanarum rerum notitia, justi atque injusti scientia. Dig. 1, 1, 1. To be skilled in law is to be conversant with things divine and human, to know the just from the unjust.

† How collected and authenticated I have been unable to ascertain.

to be Imáms, but obtained partial relief from the excessive rigidity of the sacred law in another way. It was, of course, necessary to have a staff of police and revenue officials quite distinct from the kázis, and not expected, from the nature of their ostensible duties, to have graduated in divinity. But it is never possible to separate with absolute precision administrative from strictly judicial functions; there is a natural tendency for police officers to develop into magistrates with summary jurisdiction, and for revenue officers to be called upon to decide questions of property; and whenever a lay officer took upon himself to inflict punishment or to settle a civil dispute, he would be guided partly by local usage, partly by his own common-sense, and partly by instructions from head-quarters. The amount of business disposed of according to this loose, unwritten law—called in some countries *kanoun* (regulation), in others *urf* or *zabita* (known or customary) would depend partly on local conditions, partly on the personal character of the ruler, but *ceteris paribus* would be greatest where Arabic was most completely a foreign tongue, and where the Shariat was least intelligently studied.

Differentiation of Sects and Schools.

One very natural result of this comparative absence of governmental control was that the divergences of rival schools were more marked, and also more permanent, among the Moslem ulama than among the classical jurists of Imperial Rome.

One division indeed was so deep, so embittered, and moreover so essentially political in its origin, that the legal differences involved, though intrinsically very important, cannot be regarded as by any means the chief bone of contention, and it therefore seems best to speak in this case of sects rather than of schools. I refer to the antagonism between the main body of Muhammadans, called Sunnís, and the powerful minority called Shias, the history of which

I propose to trace in the next chapter. For the present I am only concerned with the subdivisions of the Sunnís, commonly known as the four orthodox schools, namely :—

1. The Hanáfi,	founded by	Abu Hanifa,	who died A.D.	768
2. „ Máliki,	„ „	Málik Ibn Anas	„ „ „	812
3. „ Sháfaí,	„ „	Muhammad as Sháfí	„ „ „	826
4. „ Hánbalí	„ „	Ahmad Ibn Hanbal	„ „ „	863

The two first-named schools grew up independently, the one in Irák, the other at Medina. Both had been represented by able teachers before those from whom they ultimately took their names, and there is nothing to show which actually came first into existence; but as Abu Hanifa flourished somewhat earlier than Málik it will be best to begin with the former.

The Hanáfi School.

His efforts, and presumably those of his predecessors, were directed to extracting from the Koran itself more meaning than it would seem at first sight to convey, by means of what they were pleased to call analogical reasoning (*kíyás*). One or two examples may suffice to give an idea of the process.

The question propounded being whether infidels (idolaters) should be sworn in a Court of Justice, the Hanáfi answer was in the affirmative, because "all infidels believe in God;" and this rather bold generalisation was supported by the following text of the Korán :—"If ye ask of them (the infidels) who had created you, verily they will answer 'God Almighty.'"* It does not seem to have occurred to the commentator that Mahomet, or as he would say the Divine Author of the Korán, was referring to the particular infidels with whom he was then arguing, viz., the idolaters of Mecca, and that the argument in no way required a denial

* Hed. xxiv. 2. p. 405. I have been unable to find the exact text referred to. K. x. 50, xxix. 86, and xliii. 363, are something like it.

of the existence of Atheists, or of Polytheists without any notion of one supreme God.

Again, it having been declared in the Korán that "the maintenance of a woman who suckles an infant rests upon him to whom the infant is born," the Hanâfi lawyers infer *à fortiori* that the maintenance of the infant itself is incumbent on the father.*

It will easily be understood, however, that much more questionable inferences than these would be necessary in order to connect such a book as the Korán with solutions of every controversy that arose, and it was simpler to rely upon the general exhortations to justice and kindness with which it abounds, and under cover of these to deduce a considerable part of the required principles from the common necessities and feelings of mankind. How far this process may have been carried by Abu Hanifa himself I am unable to say; but certainly the Hedaya, the best known of the medieval compilations based on the teaching of his school, teems with arguments to which this description would apply.† The objection to this otherwise very convenient system is the facility with which it yields to the bias of each particular interpreter, and the consequent temptation to seek promotion by more or less ingenious accommodations of the law to the known wishes of the ruler for the time being.

Abu Hanifa himself was quite above suspicion in this respect. So far from seeking to ingratiate himself with the government of the day, he endured scourging under one dynasty and imprisonment under another rather than accept the office of Chief Kázi, which was pressed upon him, first by the last governor of Irák under the Omayads, and afterwards by the second Abbasside Caliph. The

* Hed., iv. 15. p. 146. Koran, lxvi. 18, is possibly the text referred to.

† See for instance part of the reasoning of "our doctors" in favour of a limited testamentary power, as given in the Hedaya, lii. i. p. 670; quoted in the Chapter on Wills in my "Digest."

obstinacy of both parties in these curious conflicts becomes intelligible when we remember that for each dynasty in turn it was a matter of life and death to convince their subjects that their system of government was in accordance with the Korán, which could not be done while the greatest living interpreter of the Book of God appeared to stand aloof; and that for Abu Hanifa, on the other hand, it was a certainty that as judge he would sooner or later have to choose between the deadly hatred of an earthly despot and the pains of hell-fire. The end of it was that the sturdy old man died in prison; but the fourth Abbasside, Harún al Rashid, found a more pliant instrument* in Abu Yusuf, the great disciple of Abu Hanifa, who was accordingly made Chief Kázi not only of the capital but of the empire; and so theory and practice came together in his person, as when Papinian accepted a similar office under the Roman Emperor Severus.

The third great doctor of this school, Muhammad Ibn Hasan as Shaibáni, resembled the first rather than the second in character, and for that reason never rose above a provincial judgeship.

The Máliki School.

Meanwhile the rival school had culminated at Medina, and we must now go back to trace its development. To the genuine Arabs, as distinguished from the Greek and Persian converts, and more especially to those who dwelt on the very spot which Mahomet had blessed with his presence and sanctified with his tomb, the Korán was only a part, though the central and most marvellous part, of the divine revelation with which their national greatness was identified. They neither could nor would separate the Book from the man whom they had seen with their eyes, or of whom their

* Col. Osborn ("Khalifs of Bagdad," Chap. I.) has some quaint stories illustrative of the logic by which he managed to reach the conclusions desired by his Imperial master.

fathers had told them. On the one hand, the Book spoke to them as it spoke to no foreigner, and told its own story so plainly as to leave no room for far-fetched analogical interpretations; on the other hand, the line of demarcation between what God had said through His Apostle, and what God's Apostle had said or done as an individual, would not strike them as supremely important. Hence a report found easy credence that the Prophet had said near the close of his life, "I leave with you two guides, which, if you follow faithfully, you will never go astray—the Korán and my practice (*Sunna*);"* and so the ground was prepared for building up a second fabric of law on a foundation of anecdote. Details as to this "Sunna" were, of course, easily picked up, and as easily invented, among the generation which had known the Prophet or some of his companions. In particular his favourite wife, Ayesha, who entered his harem almost an infant, and lived to an advanced age, surviving the last of the "rightly-directed Caliphs," was a most prolific source of so-called tradition. And we hear during the Omayad period of a knot of zealous Moslems known as "the seven jurists of Medina," who made it their business to utilise the biographical information obtained through this and other channels as helps to the solution of such problems of law and casuistry as from time to time presented themselves. The rules established in this way, sometimes spoken of as "the customs of Medina," at last found a systematiser in the person of Málik Ibn Anas.

This famous man, born A.D. 725, began his career as a lecturer on the traditions at the age of seventeen,† and was unremittingly employed during the remaining sixty years of

* Morley's "Digest," Introd., p. ccxxviii. The saying is hard to reconcile with the tone of the Korán itself, or with other traditions as to Mahomet's last moments, or with the fact that no measures appear to have been taken by the early Caliphs for the preservation of the Sunna similar to those taken for the preservation of the Korán.

† Von Kremer, "Culturgeschichte," I. 477.

his life on the same task, the importance of which in the eyes of his countrymen is proved by the crowds of students who came from all parts of the empire to hear him, and still more by the dignified bearing he was able to assume in presence of the Caliphs. Von Kremer aptly applies to his dwelling at Medina the saying of Cicero that "the house of the jurisconsult is the oracle of the entire community."* His chief literary work, entitled "The Beaten Path," is represented by the writer last quoted as being a veritable Corpus Juris, a comprehensive codification of the rules actually observed by upright judges and pious Moslems at Medina, all of them being of course, in his (Málik's) opinion, consistent with, if not directly sanctioned by, the Korán or the traditions. To show how entirely he rejected that exercise of natural reason under the guise of analogical deduction from the Korán, which was the favourite resource of Abu Hanifa, a saying of his is quoted that "he wished he had been flogged and reflogged every time he had ventured to give an opinion founded on his own private judgment."† He did not, however, hesitate to accept, as equivalent to a report actually traced back to the Prophet, the concurrent opinion of his leading contemporaries or predecessors at Medina, or the decisions of the "rightly-directed" Caliphs.‡

A system constructed out of such materials naturally reflected more accurately the spirit of Mahomet's own administration and the Arab modes of thought than the system excogitated by the Persian Abu Hanifa, from study of the text of the Korán by the light of his foreign prepossessions; and for that very reason the former found most favour where the population was mainly Arab, the latter among non-Arabs, such as the Persians, and, afterwards, the Turks. It was not the business of the Caliphs to pronounce authoritatively for one

* "Cic. de Oratore," I. 45.

† Osborn, "Khalifs of Bagdad," p 16.

‡ Von Kremer, "Culturgeschichte," I p. 489.

or the other; and as a matter of fact the greatest of the Abbassides, Harún al Rashíd, while he employed the Hanáfi Abu Yusuf as his Chief Kázi, yet showed Málik also the greatest attention when he happened to come to Medina on pilgrimage, and humbly sent his sons to attend Málik's class when he found that Málik was too dignified to come and give them private lessons. Yet, indirectly, the Court influence could not fail to make itself felt, and that of the Abbassides was exercised pretty constantly in favour of the Hanáfi school, for quite intelligible reasons. Their seat of government was on Persian soil; they themselves, though mainly Arab, soon came to have an admixture of Persian blood, and to lean more and more for support on Turkish troops. Perhaps, also, they may have found that courtly jurists of the type of Abu Yusuf could do more to further the private aims of the reigning sovereign under cover of the elastic phrase "analogical reasoning" than those who were pledged to the literal meanings of the Korán and the traditions.

On the other hand, the system of Málik was best liked by those Arabs who remained in their native country, and spread with the advance of Arab conquest along the North coast of Africa, where the non-Arab converts (mostly Berber) had nothing in particular to unlearn, and its predominance in North Africa would help to account for its subsequent predominance in Spain. But this last result can be traced more definitely to the political disruption of Islam in 750 A.D., and to the establishment of rival Caliphates at Bagdad and Cordova. The Hanáfi school being patronised as we have seen by the Abbassides, it was only natural that the rival system should be favoured by the rival dynasty, which represented the sole survivor from the general massacre of the Omayads, and its introduction was facilitated by the labours of a remarkable man, Yahya Ibn Yahya, who travelled from Spain to Medina for the purpose of studying personally under Málik, and whose reputation after his return caused him to be consulted on all judicial appointments. A Code of Máliki law, compiled in Spain in the 14th century A.D. by one Khalil Ibn Ishák, was found by the French to be the most authoritative source of law among their Moslem subjects in Algeria.*

The Shafai School.

The supremacy of the Hanáfi school in the Asiatic provinces of Islam was not secured as against the Málikis without very considerable concessions to the characteristic principle of the latter. Abu Hanifa himself is said to have admitted only eighteen traditions; but his successors, Abu Yusuf and Muhammad, were both accomplished traditionists, and did not disdain to confirm or supplement by anecdote the conclusions arrived at by deductive reasoning. The Hedaya, a compilation avowedly based on their teaching, is full of instances in which the two methods are combined. The instinct of endowed hierarchies, such as the *ulama* of all schools gradually became, is to think more of accumulating precedents than of cultivating a fine sense of justice, and in that competition the school which is most ostentatiously and exclusively historical cannot fail to have a certain advantage. This will partly explain how it came to pass that a third school, which accepted the fundamental principle of Málik's system, but contrived to work out of it somewhat different results, was able to wage a second contest with the Hanáfis on their own ground, not without some temporary success. As-Shafi received his early training at Mecca, under Máliki teachers, and afterwards at Medina, under Málik himself; but he was also thoroughly acquainted with the Hanáfi writings, especially with those of Muhammad, and is described by Von Kremer as being something of an eclectic,

*Translated by M. Perron, under the title "Précis de Jurisprudence Musulmane," 6 vols., Paris, 1848-1852. The second half of the work, including most of the Civil Law, but not the chapters on Marriage and Divorce, has been more recently (1878) translated by M. Seignette, under the title "Code Musulman."

though leaning more to the traditionist view. He only spent about two years of his life at Bagdad, but must have made a great impression either personally during that brief period or subsequently by his writings, as Shafite schools were common in Central Asia down to the time of the Mongol invasions; but he lived for the most part, and ultimately died, at old Cairo; and Egypt continued to be the head-quarters of his school, down to the time of the Turkish occupation,* though its supremacy was of course in abeyance during the Shia domination from 906 to 1179 A.D.

The Hanbali School.

Ahmad Ibn Hanbal is commonly spoken of as the most extreme of the traditionist Imâms; but the statement is almost unmeaning unless limited to manner as distinct from matter. In point of principle it was not possible to go beyond Málik, whose repudiation of all right of private judgment was absolute; but with him it would seem to have been the outcome of humility rather than of dogmatism, and to have meant only that he for his part would not presume to pronounce upon any question not directly covered by authority, and would confine himself to the task for which his position at Medina specially fitted him, of collecting and arranging the still fresh and fairly trustworthy evidence respecting the actual teaching and practice of Mahomet. Ibn Hanbal, on the other hand, was a combative reactionary who, living at the capital, in the full light of the most brilliant period of Arabian culture, withstood at the risk of his life the dominant spirit of rationalism in religion and of innovation in law, derided the pretensions of human reason, and pinned his faith by preference on a mass of tradition vastly more

* "Culturgesch." I. 499. As to Shafais in India, see chap. VI. *post.* I know of no European work specially devoted to this system. Numerous references to Shafai doctrines are to be found scattered about Ameer Ali's works, from which it would appear that where they diffe from the Hanáfi they most frequently agree with the Máliki, but occasionally with the Shia.

exuberant, and proportionately less authentic, than that which, in the preceding generation, had supplied the subject-matter of the "Beaten Path."

In what points of Civil Law, if any, this school differed from those of Málik and Sháfi, I have been unable to ascertain, and it would not help us much to know, inasmuch as its followers are hardly to be met with outside Arabia. The historical importance of its founder depends chiefly on the part played by him in the religious struggle between dogmatism and rationalism, which will be noticed in the next chapter.

But this seems the place for a few observations as to the tests of a valid tradition, which are apparently applied in much the same way by all the four schools.

The Traditional Method of Proving a Tradition.

The essential point is the chain of oral evidence, *isnaad.* The biographer of a modern statesman or thinker collects his facts from letters written by or to his hero, from newspapers, pamphlets, reports of speeches, in short from all kinds of documentary evidence. He must, of course, if his biography is to be worth anything, reach first-hand evidence at some point or other, but the primary witness is himself, in many cases, the author of the written or printed matter to be dealt with, and is very seldom removed from it by more than one stage of oral transmission; so that what the reader chiefly requires by way of guarantee of the biographer's good faith is merely footnotes directing him to the primary written (or printed) sources. But Mahomet wrote no letters and dictated very few; no shorthand reporters were present at his speech-makings or his judicial sittings, and we have seen that not even the divine Korán was committed to writing immediately on its delivery. Consequently the correctness of any statement as to what the Prophet had said or done could be verified in no other way than by giving the name of each person by whom it was orally transmitted. Von Kremer gives the following example from Málik's "Beaten Path."*

"Málik relates from Yahya Ibn Said, from Omra the daughter of Abd al Rahman, from Ayesha, the wife of the Prophet, who said: 'the Prophet conducted morning service, and the women returned therefrom with their upper garments wrapped round them, *in such a way that they could not be recognised in the twilight.*'"

The purpose for which the tradition is recorded is to determine the proper time for morning prayer. Málik would not have recorded it unless he had been satisfied as to the respectability of all the witnesses named. When the "Beaten Path" had become a standard text-book, it would of course no longer serve any really useful purpose to carry the chain of evidence further down; but apparently in Málik's time and long afterwards it was still contrary to etiquette to set up as a teacher of traditional lore, merely on the strength of having purchased a copy of such a work and studied it at home; the proper thing was to hear it read by the author himself or by some one under his directions, or if he were dead by some one who had so received it, and so on. †

The security obtained by this method was obviously imperfect at the best. It was, after all, only hearsay upon hearsay, and the mere fact of all the witnesses named bearing a fair character was quite consistent with any or all of them misrecollecting or misrepresenting some (possibly quite trivial) anecdote. And when we come to look closely at the original deponents, we find that Ayesha's connection with the Prophet began at the age of nine and ended before she was twenty; that she was in her later days a woman of violent prejudices, and that the reverence in which she was held as a "mother of the faithful" would in general

* "Culturgesch.," I. p. 480.

† "Culturgesch.," I. pp. 476, 482. See also II. 437.

exempt her statements from cross-examination.* Another very favourite authority, Abdallah Ibn Abbas, cousin of the Prophet, was at most fifteen years old when the latter died.

As time went on, even the imperfect test of the *isnaad* was more and more relaxed, especially in the schools which allowed no other source of law but the Korán and the traditions. Chains with one or more missing links were allowed to pass for the want of better, and the manufacture of wholly fictitious *isnaads* was found to be easy and profitable. To non-Moslems at all events the mischief will appear equally great whether the so-called traditions happened to be genuine or spurious. In either case the voice of conscience was stifled, the sense of justice perverted, and the interests of the community sacrificed, in deference to the real or supposed opinions of an ill-informed and not too immaculate Arab long dead, expressed and acted upon under widely different circumstances. Or, if anything, the most recently invented precedents had the best chance of being accommodated to modern needs.

Innovation Discountenanced. The Title of Mujtahid.

The advantage originally possessed by the Hanáfis through their partial recognition of natural reason counted for less and less as the centuries wore on. Not only were their teachers, from Abu Yusuf downwards, ambitious of displaying their acquaintance with the traditions, and of using them in support of their views whenever they could, thereby debarring themselves from repudiating such as told against them, but the authority of the earlier teachers was invoked to fetter the liberty of their successors. Whether it were owing to the increased dependence of the schools of sacred learning on endowments, or to the tendency of the

* It will be observed that in the instance above quoted the first reporter of Ayesha's statement is a woman, presumably her junior and inferior.

system to favour memory at the expense of higher gifts, or to certain other causes which will be more conveniently noticed in the next chapter, the fact seems to be that no teacher after Ibn Hanbal obtained recognition among the general body of the orthodox either as the founder of a new school or even as qualified to set his opinion on any single point against that of the founder of the school to which he had once attached himself. As Moslems would put it, no one after him was certified by the *ulama* to be a "*Mujtahid* of the first class."*

Even second-class *Mujtahids*, qualified to give independent opinions within the limits traced out by those of the first class, and third-class *Mujtahids*, standing in the same relation to the second class as those to the first, have, according to Morley, long ceased to be created among Sunni Muhammadans; but the title was still within the reach of living aspirants near the close of the 12th century of our era, if Mr. Hamilton, the translator of the Hedaya, is to be trusted when he tells us that the compiler of that work was a Mujtahid—he does not say of which class—and that he died A.H. 591 (=A.D. 1196).

Having been led to mention that famous treatise, with which the student of Anglo-Muhammadan law will have much to do, I will conclude this chapter with a brief description of it, as the readiest way of elucidating the orthodox view of the Sacred Law at the period of its fullest maturity and approaching decay.

---

* European authorities are not agreed as to the number of persons anterior to or contemporary with Ahmad Ibn Hanbal to whom the title is properly applied. Morley (Introd. p. ccxxxviii.) speaks of first-class Mujtahids as "very frequent during the first three centuries of the Hijra;" while Von Kremer ("Culturgesch." I. 504) limits it to (1) the companions of the Prophet; (2) the companions of those companions, a very vaguely-defined class; (3) the respective founders of the four chief schools and of two others now extinct; excluding therefore even the two great disciples of Abu Hanifa, whose practical equality with their master is generally recognised and acknowledged in British India.

The Hedaya.

The first thing to notice about it is the region in which it was produced. The medieval Arabs had a proverb: "Science is a tree whose root is at Mecca, but whose fruit ripens in Khorasan," and before the twelfth century A.D., some of the principal seats of learning had come to lie even further north, in the region between the Oxus and the Jaxartes, called by Arabian geographers Maweralnahr, the land beyond the river, corresponding approximately to the now Russianised Khanates of Khiva and Bokhara. Under various dynasties owing nominal allegiance to the Caliphs of Bagdad the fertile oases of this province were then made to support rich and populous cities, and in each of these were to be found colleges and libraries and competing professors of sacred and other learning. Though the political supremacy of the Arabs had long ago ebbed away from these parts, and the Turkish rulers used for most purposes the language of their Persian subjects, yet Arabic still held throughout the Moslem world, from Khokan to Cordova, a position corresponding to that of Latin in Western Christendom as the universal language of law and religion; and it was in that language that one, Sheikh Burhan-ud-Din Ali, of Marghinan, composed first a treatise called the Badáyat, which seems to have been found too difficult for ordinary students, and then an expanded paraphrase of the same which obtained a wider and more lasting reputation under the name of the Hedaya.* It was about the time when Richard of England and Saladin were contending in Syria, and not far from the date fixed by English lawyers for the commencement of "legal memory." While the English common law was just beginning to take shape, the Muhammadan Law had reached a point at which all idea of

* *Hedaya fil foru*, *i.e.*, guide to the "branches," or detailed applications, of the "roots" or fundamental principles. See Hamilton's "Hedaya," Pref. DIX. p. xxvi.

substantial improvement had been abandoned, and a neater re-statement of established doctrines was the highest thing aimed at.

The doctrines re-stated are those of the Hanáfi school, on all the subjects included in the Shariat. The first of four volumes is occupied with the purely religious duties of Purification, Prayer, Alms, Fasting, and Pilgrimage; the other three volumes deal chiefly with what we should consider secular topics, though even here we find an entire book about "vows" interposed between the law of divorce and the criminal law, and in the fourth volume, between "compacts of gardening" and "cultivation of waste lands," we have disquisitions on the proper mode of killing animals, on sacrifice, and on what the translator calls Abominations, *i.e.*, acts which, though not illegal, are unbecoming.*

The compiler's general plan is to state on each point the opinion of "our doctors," noting on occasion the divergent opinions of Málik and Sháfi, and also the differences between Abu Hanifa and one or both of the "two disciples."† The arguments on either side, whether derived from the Korán, from the traditions, or from natural reason, are stated with an appearance of impartiality, and we can only rather doubtfully infer that the compiler himself is on the side of the disputant whom he allows to have the last word. Sometimes the authority relied on is a decree passed without objection in presence of the companions of the Prophet, which is perhaps the most proper signification of the vague expression *ijmaa* (concurrence), when employed to denote a fourth source of law co-ordinate with the Korán, the traditions, and *Kiyas*. In no case, so far as I have observed, is any decision of a Caliph, other than the four "rightly-directed," referred to as a source of law.

---

* *E.g.*, eating hare's flesh. See an anecdote in Malcolm's "Persia," vol. II., p. 432.

† Abu Yusuf and Muhammad.

For the purpose of understanding what kind of law followed in the wake of the Moslem invaders of India, we may very well stop with the publication of the Hedaya. The regions of Central Asia, from or through which these invaders entered Hindustán, were swept, a quarter of a century later, by the first of the terrible Mongol invasions. About 1220 the hordes of Zingis Khan wiped the rich and populous cities of Transoxiana clean out of existence, "massacring everywhere all classes except the artisans, of whom they made slaves."* It is true that the successors of Zingis made this very country their head-quarters, re-peopling it therefore to the extent implied in a vast army and a splendid court, and enriching it with the spoils of other conquests; that some of them were fairly cultured and humane, and that even those who were most ruthless on the warpath liked to surround themselves with men of learning; and that when (from 1295 A.D.), they began to adopt the religion of their subjects, the schools of the Sacred Law received a full share of their patronage, and flourished in a way as long as the Tartar dynasties themselves. But the conditions were even more unfavourable to independent research and innovation than those under which the Hedaya was produced; and as a matter of fact nothing of the kind seems to have been attempted, except perhaps among the Shias, whose development will be traced in the next chapter.

* Milman's footnote to Gibbon ("Decl. and Fall," viii. 8), from D'Ohsson's "Histoire des Mongols."

APPENDIX TO CHAPTER II.

Muhammadan Law Viewed in the Light of Austin's Analysis of Law and Sovereignty.

THE German writer to whom I am indebted for so much of the matter of this chapter, was not embarrassed by a difficulty which has to be faced by one who writes primarily for students trained according to the modern English system of legal education. Von Kremer could compare the development of the idea of Law (Recht) by Arabs and Romans without any apprehension of being charged with using the same word in two different senses. A disciple of Austin is bound to ask, Was this Muhammadan Shariat true positive law, or mere positive morality, or a system of divine law, sometimes coinciding and sometimes conflicting with the contemporary positive law? To this I should answer that, those who were responsible for building up the Shariat would have repudiated Austin's definition, had it been propounded in their time; but, nevertheless, the system did in great part, under the Caliphs of Bagdad, and does still under the Sultan of Turkey, practically satisfy that definition, though in an indirect and not immediately obvious manner.

Readers of the "Province of Jurisprudence"* will remember that the definition requires in the first place a "sovereign," *i.e.*, a person or body of persons, receiving habitual obedience from the bulk of the community, and

* See especially Lecture VI., Vol. I., p. 226 (p. 82 of the "Student's Austin").

not habitually obeying any determinate human superior, and requires in the next place that this sovereign should not merely order this or that to be done, but should lay down more or less permanent rules for the conduct of his subjects, which rules then become "positive law" by the definition. Now the Moslems considered themselves bound in conscience to obey the Caliph only in so far as his commands were in accordance with the divine law, and they looked to such teachers as Abu Hanífa and Málik to tell them what the divine law was. So did the Caliph himself.

No obedience, in the Austinian sense of the term, was rendered to Abu Hanífa in Irák, or to Málik in Arabia and Spain. That is to say, those saintly men never took upon themselves to order the punishment of any one for non-compliance with their wishes. Austin could not possibly have regarded the Mujtahíds as exercising authority over, or even as sharing it with, the Caliph. He must either have declared the Caliph to be sovereign, or else have declared the Moslem community to be in a state of anarchy, by reason of their obedience to the Commander of the Faithful being avowedly dependent on their individual opinion as to the religious propriety of his commands. If he adopted the latter alternative, he would have had to exclude all other communities of conscientious and God-fearing men from the category of political societies, thereby making his whole system ridiculous. The difficulty disappears if we are careful to remember that sovereignty with Austin is a pure question of fact, depending on the ordinary behaviour of the bulk of the given community. A devout Moslem at Medina might theoretically, and, no doubt, sometimes did practically, find himself between two fires, the Caliph's officers ordering him to do what according to Málik he ought not to do. But, in general, one of three things would happen. Either (1) the Caliph, knowing the extent of Málik's spiritual influence, and perhaps himself fearing divine punishment if he set himself against the divine law as enunciated by those best acquainted with it, would abstain from issuing orders which would involve him in such a conflict, and therefore it would remain true that he issued no orders which were not obeyed; or (2) the bulk of his subjects, being more afraid of the master of legions in the present than of hell-fire in the future, would stifle their conscientious objections and do as they were told, while the minority would either passively suffer martyrdom or be crushed in unsuccessful rebellion; or (3) the Moslems generally, or the more influential portion of them, would side with Málik, in which case rebellion would have become revolution, and a new Caliph, governing in harmony with the accepted expositors of the divine law, would again, after a brief interval of anarchy, fully satisfy the definition of *de facto* sovereignty.

Each of these suppositions may be illustrated from the history of the period. The first represents, of course, the normal state of things, specially exemplified in Spain, when Yahya, after his return from his course of study under Málik, was consulted by the Caliph of Cordova as to the appointment of Kazís throughout his dominions, and recommended only those trained in the Máliki system. The second may be illustrated by the case of Málik himself, when he ventured to express the opinion that the house of Ali had a better right to the Caliphate than the then reigning Omayad dynasty. A rebellion took place at Medina, in which he took no part; after its suppression, he was scourged and otherwise tortured to make him retract his opinion, but, remaining firm, was ultimately let alone. He survived by many years the dethronement of the dynasty which persecuted him, an event which may serve to exemplify our third supposition. He taught freely, and was treated with respect under four Abbasside Caliphs, and it was apparently open to any Kazi to decide according to his opinion if he thought fit, though the Caliphs themselves, in matters judicially before them, or in their private affairs of conscience, preferred to consult more congenial advisers, and the fourth

Abbasside in particular enabled Abu Yúsuf, as his Chief Justice, to fill the Bench with Kâzis of the Hanáfi persuasion. Thus the sovereignty of Harún Al Rashíd was secured partly by his conforming his orders to the opinions of the leading lawyers, and partly by some of them moulding their opinions to suit his known wishes.

But the question remained—granting the Caliph to have been sovereign, was he a legislating sovereign? Or, to be more exact (for there is no doubt as to *some* ordinances of a more or less permanent character having emanated directly from the Caliphs), can we properly speak of the Shariat, or Sacred Law, as an enactment proceeding from the Caliph for the time being?

I think Austin would have so regarded it, though the Caliph himself probably would not. Austin would have asked simply, what temporal penalties (if any) were to be expected as the consequence of violating a rule of the Shariat, and on what human will did their enforcement depend? In some cases, *e.g.*, the omission of an able-bodied Moslem to perform the pilgrimage to Mecca, no temporal penalties at all would ensue. But suppose a Moslem guilty of drinking wine. According to a precept of the Prophet recorded by tradition, he ought to be scourged. But if the Caliph, or his deputy the Kazi, refuses to inflict this punishment—as in practice not unfrequently happened—the supposed rule of law becomes a dead letter; and a dead letter does not come within the Austinian definition of law as "a general command proceeding from a superior who intends to inflict punishment in case of non-compliance." It follows that if the punishment is inflicted, or if the Moslems of Bagdad are given to understand that it will be inflicted in future, the rule of the Shariat, of which the Caliph considers himself a humble minister, is, in fact, his law. Though nominally only the executive head of the State, he is in reality the legislative head also. His acknowledgment of a divine law to which he must conform is common to all legislative bodies composed wholly or chiefly of professedly religious men. But whereas the British Parliament, reflecting the general state of opinion in the British nation, admits a very large range of uncertainty as to what the divine law really prescribes, looks forward rather than backward for further enlightenment, and decides for itself all doubtful points so far as is necessary for its own limited purposes, the Caliphs of Bagdad, reflecting the general Moslem opinion, believed (with one exception to be noticed in the next chapter) in an all-embracing divine law to be collected from a single book and a single biography, and were content to adopt as their own the conclusions of those whom they perceived to have the highest reputation for knowledge of these two sources. Differing on this point from a well-known jurist,* I consider that it *does* "conduce to clear thinking" to look occasionally behind the conventional phraseology of theocratic jurisprudence, and to put one's finger on the hidden point of junction between the political and the religious sanction.

* Maine's "Early History of Institutions," p. 385. "How can it conduce to clear thinking to speak of the Jewish law as having been commanded at one period by the Great King at Susa?" I might answer that it would help us to understand what many people regard as the central event of human history, the enforcement of the Jewish law of blasphemy by the Roman governor, Pontius Pilate.

CHAPTER III.

UNORTHODOX DEVELOPMENT OF MUHAMMADAN LAW. THE MOTAZALAS AND THE SHIAS.

"Out of the frying-pan into the fire."—OLD SAW.

IT has been shown in the preceding chapter that, according to the view taken by the bulk of professing Moslems as to the nature of the revelation vouchsafed to Mahomet, it covered the whole field of law as well as of theology, and when once historical research had brought together all that was ever likely to be known concerning the life and teaching of God's Apostle, and commentators had extracted and set in order the rules of civil law deducible therefrom, there was really no further room for development, except in the way of working out the rules so established into more and more minute ramifications. But though the main current of opinion has set steadily in this direction from the first publication of the Korán to the present day, there have not been wanting vigorous efforts on the part of influential minorities to open out new channels of religious thought and aspiration, and incidentally to modify the corresponding rules of law and ethics.

The Motázalas.

The simplest method of attaining this object was to treat the Koranic revelation as a message addressed primarily to Mahomet's contemporaries and countrymen, not necessarily suited in all respects to a different age and a different state of society. From the position taken up by the Hanáfi school, the left wing (so to speak) of orthodoxy, that in default of direct guidance from the Korán or trustworthy tradition there was room for the exercise of natural reason at least in the way of "analogical deduction," it was not so very long a step to assert that Mahomet was only a person divinely appointed to direct special attention to certain truths which were being ignored, and that other portions of divine truth, or even the same truths, might reveal themselves in a natural way to any honest and open mind. Some such view is said to have been put forward by a sect called the Kadarites during the latter half of the Omayad period, in support of their doctrine of free will as against the gloomy fatalism deduced from the Korán by the majority of expounders; but it was more effectively championed under the first Abbasside by Wásil Ibn Ata, who earned the nickname of Motázala (Separatist) by formally separating himself from his teacher, Hásán Basri, on a somewhat cognate question.*

The Baneful Patronage of Al Mámún.

Half a century later his followers, still known as Motázalas, found themselves in the full sunshine of Court favour under the Caliph Al Mámún (813-833). This was far from being an unmixed advantage for the cause of reform, either religious or legal. The Caliph combined, like our own Henry VIII. and James I., the keenest speculative interest in great subjects, and among others in religion, with less than the average of moral principle.† A poisoner and fratricide,‡ and stained with other odious

* Von Kremer, "Gesch.," II. 409-413; Osborn, "Khalifs of Bagdad," chap. iv.

† Muir, "The Caliphate," chap. lxv., pronounces rather favourably as to his general character as a sovereign; but the facts faithfully recorded by himself suggest a very different estimate.

‡ This can hardly be imputed as a crime to a Muhammadan ruler. It is rather an extraordinary merit to avoid either killing or blinding a brother who, whether older or younger, has precisely as good a right as yourself to the throne, with no possible arbiter but the sword, and who will by law exclude your sons from the succession, should he survive you without being physically incapacitated from reigning. In this particular case Amín rather than Mámún was the aggressor.

crimes, he was at the same time the most liberal patron of literature and philosophy. He gathered round him for amicable discussion representatives of all the leading religions and of all contemporary modes of thought, and delighted especially in the conversation of one Ibn Abi Douad, a follower of Wásil. The effect of such influences being brought to bear on such a sovereign was that he could think of no better way of promoting free inquiry than that of persecuting those who objected to it. Himself probably a thorough sceptic at heart, he not only exercised but strained his authority as Defender of the Faith in order to punish its genuine defenders when he thought he had caught them tripping through excess of zeal. Some of the orthodox had sought to strengthen their case against the rationalists by asserting that the Korán must have existed from all eternity exactly as it was delivered by Mahomet. The Rationalists retorted rather unfairly, that this was to set up in some sort a second Deity and thus to infringe the fundamental principle of Islam. Al Mámún accepted this view, and established a special Court of Inquisition to deal with the "heresy" of maintaining that the Korán was uncreated. This same monarch also made it pretty clear what sort of reformer he would be if he were allowed to revise by his own authority the accepted interpretations of the sacred law. On one occasion he took upon himself to issue an edict declaring *mota*, *i.e.*, temporary, marriages to have been sanctioned by the Prophet, but recoiled before the determined opposition of the Sunnì jurists. His defeat was the more remarkable, because the point was one upon which there was really a conflict of authorities, and the Shia lawyers were on his side. But in Islam as in Christendom he who would attack deeply-rooted superstitions with success must come to the task with clean hands and a faith in something better, and the example of Pope Leo X. was about as likely to commend the culture of the renaissance to popular favour as was that of Mámún to gain acceptance for Rationalism with simple-minded earnest Moslems. The Motázalas had no Luther ; at most only a faint anticipation of Wyclif in Wásil Ibn Ata, and some dubious counterparts of Erasmus among the court favourites of Al Mámún. What plain Englishmen felt about Henry VIII.'s Reformation scheme, when they saw it heralded by the royal divorce and followed by the execution of More, would be felt in a measure by the average Moslem of Bagdad, when he saw men like Ahmad Ibn Hanbal, of enormous (even if useless) learning and undoubted piety, beaten and imprisoned for thinking more highly of Mahomet and the Korân than seemed proper to a government which was suspected of wishing to get rid of the Korân altogether.

The Reaction.

Rationalism managed to maintain a precarious official supremacy through what remained of Al Mámún's reign and those of the two next Caliphs, making together about thirty years, but the reaction was all this time gathering force, and at last Mutawákkil, the third successor of Al Mámún, awoke to the fact that as a scourge of heretics he would have the bulk of the population* on his side, while as a supporter of Rationalism and of the penal law against the doctrine of an uncreated Koran he would have only his Turkish mercenaries *plus* a few unpopular literati. He chose accordingly, and the Motázalas, persecuted in their turn, sank rapidly into obscurity ; and though we hear of some remarkably free religious discussions, even in Bagdad itself, about a century later, I am not aware that the Motázalas as a sect were heard of again until their recent revival under the shelter of British rule. Ahmad Ibn Hanbal lived to see the

* *i.e.*, the population of Bagdad and vicinity, mostly Arab. How it was in the regions of Khorassan and Transoxiana, now nearly independent of the Caliphs and of Arab ascendancy under the Tahiride dynasty, I am unable to say.

cause for which he endured so much completely triumphant, and history records that when he died, A.D. 863, 860,000 persons attended his funeral, and 20,000 infidels were "miraculously" converted—a miracle not difficult to account for, considering the disabilities and oppressions from which, under the new régime, conversion offered the only escape.

The Shias.

After the failure of rationalism to commend itself to the general body of Moslems, and the consequent extinction of all hope of loosening at any point the rigid Koranic framework of the Shariat by means of suggestions that the Prophet's injunctions might be of only local and temporary application, there yet remained one way in which Islam might possibly modify its laws without ceasing to be Islam.

It has been shown (p. 17) that Mahomet in his lifetime was continually receiving new revelations, the later sometimes even abrogating the earlier, and that the faithful were sorely puzzled by the question why Allah should have suddenly taken His Apostle to Himself while the series was still unfinished. Now, what if the Almighty had after all made provision for the perpetual presence among men of a living channel of inspiration which they in their blindness had overlooked? And where was such a living oracle more naturally to be looked for than in the line of the Prophet's descendants?

Meaning of the Term.

Such was the view which began to find favour with a considerable, though scattered and disunited, minority towards the close of the first century of Islam, and at a somewhat later period its votaries came to be known collectively by the name "Shia." The word means literally a follower, or partisan, and thus designates not inaptly the characteristic of devotion to a *person,* in contradistinction to the Sunni, or orthodox Moslem, whose piety consists in conformity to the *routine* sanctified by the precept and example of the Prophet.

As to the particular person who was to be regarded at any given time as the living representative of God and His Apostle, there were many differences of opinion among the Shias, to explain which we must go back to the origin of the movement.

Origin and Grounds of the Pretensions of the House of Ali.

Whatever the Shias may pretend, many considerations render it practically certain that no notion of a right of succession to the Caliphate, still less to the prophetic function, can have entered the head of any responsible person until many years after the death of Mahomet. The Arab sentiment was republican if anything, though they had no practical experience of any form of regular government; and, what is more important, there was no descendant of the Prophet upon whom his mantle could at that time without absurdity be supposed to have fallen. The only child who survived him was his daughter Fátima, whose sons, Hassan and Husain, were mere infants. His nearest collateral blood relation was his uncle Abbas, who had been but a tardy and lukewarm supporter of the cause, though personally friendly to his nephew, and always treated by him with respect. Next in proximity of blood, and much closer in affection, stood his cousin Ali, son of his favourite uncle, husband of his favourite daughter, almost his earliest convert, and one of the bravest and gentlest of his warriors. He certainly never pretended to any prophetic gift, probably was never thought of as a competitor against Abu Bakr or Omar for the Caliphate, or, if he was, his claim was purely personal, not hereditary. He was a competitor at the third election, but was postponed to Othman, Mahomet's other son-in-law—tradition says because he would not promise to be bound by the decisions of his two predecessors, but only by the Korán and Mahomet's own example. Othman's misgovernment ended after six years in a rebellion which cost him his life. Then Ali, whose efforts at mediation had been baffled by the obstinacy and treachery of Othman,* at last became Caliph by the suffrages of the Arabs at Medina, who would include, and perhaps largely consist of, the rebels who were more or less directly responsible for the death of his predecessor. His enemies, and the partisans of the late Caliph, were not slow to take advantage of this, and the result was that, notwithstanding his far higher character and ability, his reign was even more troubled than that of his predecessor, and had an equally violent ending. His sovereignty was at no time acknowledged in the two great provinces of Syria and Egypt, and was maintained with difficulty elsewhere; ultimately, after much confused fighting and negotiation, he was forced to make a formal cession of those provinces to their respective governors, who had held them ever since they were placed there by his predecessor; and when he fell by the hand of an assassin, the claim of his eldest son, Hassan, to succeed him was but feebly asserted, and easily set aside. Then Muáwia, the governor of Syria, assumed the undivided Caliphate without any form of election and with little opposition, removed the seat of government from Medina to Damascus, and became the founder of that Omayad dynasty of which I have already had occasion to speak. What now concerns us is the way in which this ambitious ruler set about changing the Caliphate from a nominally elective to a partially hereditary office. He assumed the right of nominating a successor among the members of his own family, and required all Moslems of any consequence to swear prospective allegiance to his son Yezíd. The elective system had worked so badly that most acquiesced for the sake of peace and quiet; but among the few who refused at the risk of their lives was Husain, the

* This is the more favourable view, taken by Colonel Osborn. Sir William Muir and Von Kremer represent him as secretly fomenting the rebellion from the very first. Muir, "Caliphate," p. 240, 301. Kremer, "H. I.," p. 352.

younger son of Ali and Fátima. The elder, Hassan, was by this time dead; the Shias assert that he was poisoned by Muáwia.

The Massacre of Kerbela, and its Consequences.

Nothing happened at the time; but some twenty years later, when Muáwia died, and Yezíd actually assumed the Caliphate, Husain was encouraged to assert his claim in arms. In point of justice his claim was certainly a strong one. If the new idea that the office should be hereditary was sound, who should have a better right than the son of the last elected Caliph, and the grandson (in the female line, it is true) of the Prophet himself? While, if it was elective, he had at least a good right as Yezíd to offer himself to the suffrages of the faithful. But, wherever the right lay, the might proved to be on the other side. Husain did not meet with the support he expected, and in the open plain of Kerbela, he and a small band of followers, including nearly the whole of his family, were surrounded by an overwhelming force and massacred to a man (A.D. 680.)

The shock to Moslem sentiment may be imagined. That within half a century of the death of God's Apostle his grandson and great-grandsons should be done to death by the myrmidons of a self-constituted Commander of the Faithful, who was himself, moreover, a grandson of Mahomet's leading opponent, was calculated to array against him all who seriously believed the accepted creed of Islam. And there are many indications that it actually had that effect, not only during the short remainder of Yezíd's reign, but during the whole subsequent existence of the Omayad dynasty, a period of about seventy years. Rebellion was chronic, and though other sects and parties had their share, still, a very large proportion of the disturbances had for object or pretext the restoration of the House of Ali. Moreover, pious and learned men, who kept quite aloof from tumults and civil war, did not hesitate on occasion to express opinions unfavourable to the reigning dynasty. We cannot yet speak of a distinct Alyite, or Shia party, because sympathy, more or less pronounced, with the misfortunes and aspirations of the descendants of the Prophet was a normal accompaniment of orthodoxy. The fact that, in spite of this consensus of pious aversion, the Omayads managed to hold their own for so long a period, is a striking proof of the length to which what may be called the secularisation of Islam had proceeded. War and conquest, from being the means of propagating a purer faith, had come to be ends in themselves, the means to which consisted much more in statecraft, organising power, and military ability, than in religious enthusiasm. Those who took their religion seriously either engaged in insurrections which were uniformly unsuccessful and ruthlessly punished, or escaped the dull tyranny within by fighting against the infidel beyond the frontiers, or devoted themselves to the study and interpretation of the sacred law; a department with which, as was shown in Chap. II., the Caliphs wisely abstained from interfering. This last was the resource to which some of the best representatives of the House of Ali betook themselves, while others asserted their claim in arms, and got killed for their pains. The origin and divisions of the Shia sect cannot be understood without examining these cases individually. The genealogical Table set out on the opposite page will be found useful for reference.

Divisions among the Fatimides.

Only one infant son of Husain escaped the massacre of Kerbela. He was named Ali (No. 4) after his grandfather, but was distinguished in after ages by the epithet Zain-ul-Abidín ("Ornament of the Pious"). His mother was a daughter of the last king of Persia, so that besides his claims on the allegiance of Moslems as such, he had a special hold on the affections of converted and unconverted Persians.

GENEALOGY TO ILLUSTRATE THE DYNASTIC CLAIMS OF THE SHIAS AND THEIR RIVALS.

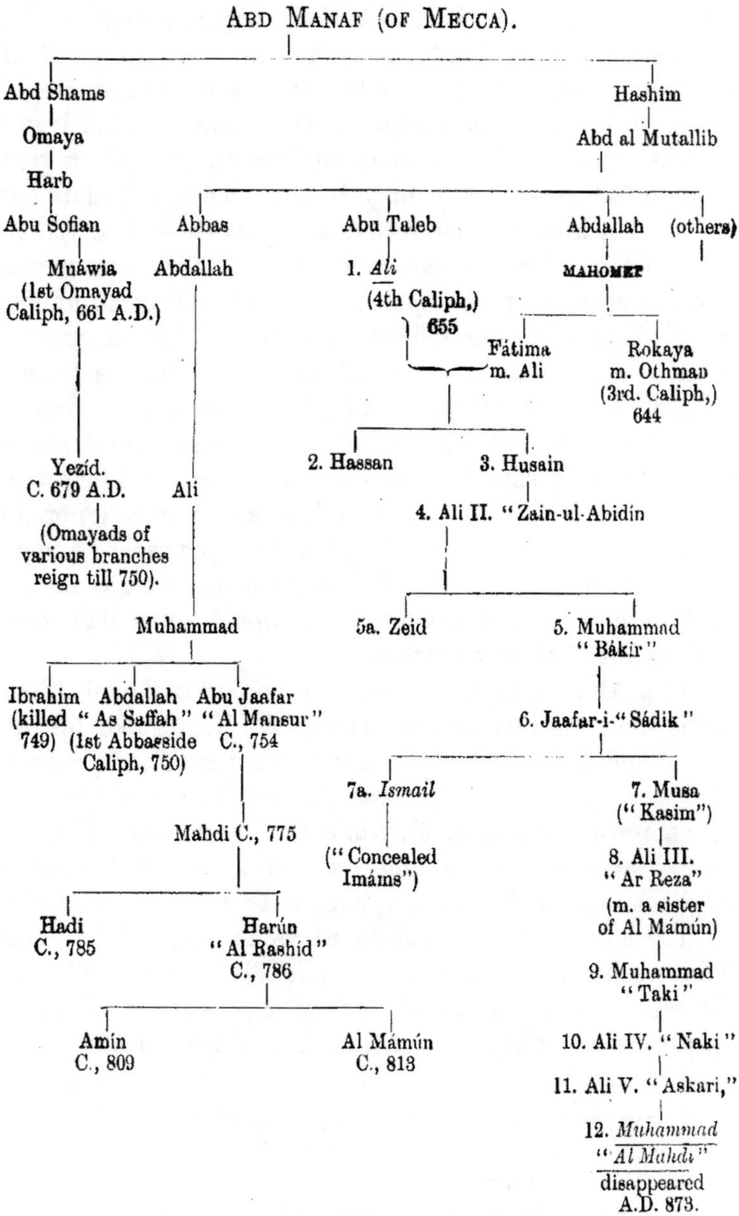

Thus those who fully accepted the hereditary principle,* but were disposed to turn it against the usurping Omayads who had invented it, looked upon this Ali (No. 4) as their sovereign *de jure*, whatever reluctant obedience they might render to the *de facto* Caliph at Damascus. But Ali was (as I have said) an infant when his father died. The notion of an infant ruler was strange to the Arab mind, and that of an infant leader of opposition must have been if anything, still more so. The succession of brothers to the exclusion of infant sons is a familiar expedient in all rude communities and ultimately became a fixed principle of Moslem government. Hence a fraction of the opposition attached themselves to one Muhammad (Ibn al Hanafiya) a son of the Caliph Ali, but not by Fátima, as being the natural successor of Husain, and as near as anyone in kinship to the Prophet, if descent through a female were to be ignored.† He died in 700 A.D., but the belief was long cherished among his followers that he was kept miraculously alive in the recesses of a mountain, whence he would some day come forth and lead them to victory.‡

As for Ali Zain-ul-Abidín, he took no part in the rebellions of the time, but received in private the homage of his disciples, and gave them advice in matters of faith and practice. The same peaceful policy was pursued by one of his sons, Muhammad Bakir (No. 5), while the other, Zeid (No. 5A), headed an insurrection and was slain. A small sect of Zeidians survives to this day, but the true line of succession is generally traced by modern Shias through Muhammad Bakir to his more famous son (No. 6) Jaafar-i-Sádik (the righteous) who combined with a reputation for saintly gentleness and piety that of an acknowledged master of the

* The party which adhered to the old republican ideal had a stirring history of its own, which does not now concern us.

† As to this see Chap. vi.

‡ Von Kremer, "Herrschenden ideen des Islams," p. 377.

sacred law. Abu Hanífa himself was originally his disciple, though he afterwards took an independent line.

The Abbassides.

This Jaafar died about A.D. 776,* and thus lived to see the event so long prayed for by devout Moslems generally and his followers in particular. In 750 A.D. sudden and utter ruin overtook the detested Omayads,† but he does not appear to have taken any part in the business, and politically his party was very little, if at all, better off in consequence of it. The leadership of the attempt which proved successful after so many failures fell, as it happened, by virtue of superior aptitude for the rough work of revolution, to the representatives of Abbas, the paternal uncle, instead of to the lineal descendants of the Prophet.

According to Arab notions of inheritance, which took very small account of descent through females, there was almost as much to be said for the former as for the latter; and in point of fact the bulk of the Arab race bowed readily enough—for the moment at least—to the accomplished fact, including a section of the Alyites, who gave credence to a tale that the son and successor of Muhammad Ibn al Hanafiya (p. 60) had abdicated in favour of the then representative of the House of Abbas, the father of the three brothers who, actually conducted the final struggle. But on the other hand the House of Ali had commanded the almost undivided attachment of the Persians, in whose country the revolt commenced, and on whose support it had in its earlier stages mainly depended. The conversion of these Persians was in many cases only skin-deep, and even where it was genuine they read the Korán as a foreign book, missed the true spirit of its austere monotheism, and were

---

* Osborn, "Islam under the Arabs," p. 168. I do not know whence he derives the statement.

† With exception of one member of the family, who long afterwards founded a rival Caliphate in Spain.

apt to conceive of Mahomet as a Divine Incarnation, or at least (in fire-worshipping phrase) as "a ray of the Divine effulgence." At the same time they felt a more real and living interest in Ali and Husain than in Mahomet himself; in Ali, because his brief reign had given them a governor whose rule was remembered as a halcyon interval between two long periods of Arab oppression;* and in Husain, because of his connection with their ancient royal line, and his tragic death on their soil at the hands of their enemies. Out of hatred to the Omayads they engaged in the struggle without any clear understanding for which branch they were really fighting; but hoping no doubt that some share at least of the fruits of victory would fall to their party. As a nation, they were not wholly disappointed. The new seat of government was planted at Bagdad, within their borders, and there Persian began at once to contend with Arab influences on not altogether unequal terms, growing more powerful as time went on. But the partisans of the House of Ali were no better off than before. When once the Omayads were disposed of, the main body of the Arabs still organised as a great military caste, concentrated in the new capital and other commanding positions, gave their support to the competitors in possession, and the dynastic question being one on which there was no room for compromise, the weaker party had only the choice between passive acquiescence and a life of underground plotting with occasional desperate outbreaks.

Roughly speaking, these were the sharply-contrasted policies of the two sections into which the Alyites (or Shias, as they had now at all events come to be called) divided themselves after the death of Jaafar-i-Sádik.

The Ismailian Shias.

The story is that this saintly person found his eldest son Ismail (No. 7A) drunk, and thereupon disinherited him in

* Muir's "Caliphate," p. 293.

favour of his younger son, Musa (Kasim, No. 7); that one section of the party accepted this decision, while the other section maintained that the succession according to primogeniture was a matter of inalienable divine right, and that the appointed guide to the consciences of the faithful could not possibly do wrong.

And it must here be observed that the dignity in dispute was not, in Shia phraseology, the Caliphate, but the Imâmate, in their view something vastly greater, involving full power to bind and loose in this world and the next. In the case of the Ismailian Shias this view had extremely practical consequences.

Devoted body and soul to their Imâm, and ready at any moment to kill or be killed at his bidding, they rendered him so extremely formidable a person that no government acquainted with his name and whereabouts would have tolerated his existence for a month. For this reason all the successors of Ismail, whom they reckoned as the seventh Imâm, were *concealed*, and from their concealment instigated, or were supposed to instigate, sudden and desperate blows every now and then at unguarded points of the Empire. Thus small Shia dynasties sprang into existence at various points along the north coast of Africa, where the rude Berbers resembled the polished Persians in covering their hatred of Arab rule under pretext of attachment to some new version of the faith of Islam. These small successes were followed in course of time by the far more important conquest of Egypt, which was ruled by a Fátimite dynasty, descendants of Ismail, from A.D. 908 to 1179. Here the extreme Shia theory—that the veritable Imâm is the absolute representative of God upon earth, was thoroughly put to the test of practice, with the result that relief from the dull pressure of Sunní routine and from the pedantic intolerance of the Ulama, were felt to be on the whole too dearly purchased at the cost of such freaks of tyranny as were indulged in by the third and most famous of these semi-divine beings.* There must have been some merit, at least as compared with the not too high standard of contemporary orthodox Islam, in a dynasty which lasted so long and left behind it so splendid a monument as the city of Cairo; but, on the whole, the orthodox were not far wrong in regarding this beautiful capital as a hotbed of mischief, and the re-conquest of Egypt by the famous Saladin (who was a zealous Sunní of the school of As Sháfi) as a service at least equally meritorious with his recovery of Jerusalem from the Crusaders.

The Assassins.

One well-known product of this hotbed would have amply sufficed to justify the general sentiment even had it stood alone, which was very far from being the case. Among the missionaries constantly sent out from Egypt into Central Asia to preach the Ismailian doctrines and to foment conspiracies against the various governments more or less connected with the Caliphate of Bagdad, was one Hasan Ibn Sabah, who contrived amidst the confusions of the time to possess himself of an almost inaccessible castle near the Caspian, and to acquire so marvellous an ascendancy over the minds of the followers who there gathered round him, that he could send them out with secret orders to kill any person in any part of the world, and could perfectly rely on the attempt being made at all risks and in face of every obstacle. Some eight "Grand Masters" carried on this extraordinary system through upwards of a century and a half (1090-1258) sometimes on such a scale as to count among the great powers of Asia, and always with sufficient effect to cause widespread misery and terror, until at last they were extirpated, almost simultaneously with the Caliphate of Bagdad, by a still more terrible scourge of humanity in the shape of the second Mongol invasion under Hulagu Khan.

* Osborn, "Islam under the Arabs," p. 250.

It is, of course, idle to look for reforms of the Shariat in the history of a community of murderers, but it may be worth mentioning that the later Grand Masters, after the overthrow of the Fátimite power in Egypt, claimed to be themselves descendants of Ismail and veritable Imâms, and in that character one of them is said to have expressly repealed the Koranic prohibitions against wine-drinking, gambling, and other vices, and, indeed, the moral law generally. The last Grand Master, on the other hand, re-established the ordinary forms of religion, and was anxious to be recognised as an orthodox Moslem. From the extirpation of the "Assassins" the Ismailian Shias cease to play a conspicuous part in history, though members of the sect are still to be found in various parts of the world, and, among other places, in Western India.*

The Isna-Asharya Shias.

That branch of the Shia party which followed Musa Kasim ("the patient") in preference to Ismail, pursued under the Abbassides a less ambitious policy, but for that very reason struck deeper roots and exercised a more lasting influence. Six Imâms in succession, following the example of Jaafar-i-Sádik, lived openly and quietly under the eye of the Bagdad Caliphs; sometimes suffering under the not unnatural jealousy of the Government, as when Musa himself (No. 7) died in prison under Harún al Rashíd, and Ali V. (No. 11) under Mutawákkil; sometimes negotiated with almost on equal terms, as when Al Mámún gave his own sister in marriage to Ali, the son of Musa, and proposed to make him his successor; a step prompted by the Caliph's Persian sympathies and by his hatred of the orthodox party, but retracted as soon as it was seen to be unpopular, and atoned for by the poisoning of his unfortunate brother-in-law. At last, one Muhammad, the sixth from Jaafar,

* This account is chiefly taken from Osborn's "Islam under the Arabs," Part II, Chap. IV., and "Khalifs of Baghdad," Part III, Chap. III.

reckoned as the twelfth of the entire series, hunted by the satellites of the Government, suddenly disappeared, and thereby gave his followers an excuse for disembarrassing themselves once for all from the inconvenient obligation of allegiance to a living depository of divine inspiration, who might at one time be incapable of defending his subjects and at another time only too capable of oppressing them. It became an article of belief that this Muhammad "Al Mahdi" ("the expected one"), as he was now called, was miraculously kept alive, though invisible and unapproachable, that he would reappear in power at the appointed time to set everything straight, and that meanwhile the faithful must get on as best they could with the guidance of the Korán, the traditions, and the precepts and example of the twelve recognised Imâms—whence the name Isna-Asharya ("Twelvers") by which they are distinguished from the Ismailians.

Triumph of the Shia Faith in Persia.

After this new departure, and indeed to some extent before it, owing to the generally unassuming attitude of their Imâms, these Isna-Asharya Shias were almost as much concerned as the Sunnís to work out a complete system of doctrine, ritual, and civil and criminal law, for the guidance of their members, and in order to commend their principles to outsiders; and ample materials for this purpose lay ready to their hands, in the works of Jaafar-i-Sádik and his more or less learned successors, with the commentaries of admiring disciples. They were also free to utilise, as provisional deputy for the absentee Imám, any able leader who might happen to arise, or any established ruler who might be disposed to patronise them, without raising any question of hereditary right. Accordingly, this form of the Shia faith was at different times openly espoused by the vizier of a puppet Caliph of Bagdad, and by one or two Tartar princes; and at last, about the date considered by Europeans to mark the transition from mediæval to modern history, an opportunity occurred of solidly establishing it as the State religion of what has ever since been known as Persia: an area corresponding roughly with the Western half of the old Sassanide Empire, occupied by such a mixture of Turks, Arabs, and Persians as only a distinctive belief could have welded into a distinct and fairly compact nationality.

The name of the founder of this new order of things, Ismail, would suggest a connection with the Ismailian Shias, but in point of fact he claimed to be a remote descendant of Musa, the seventh Imám according to the Isna-Asharyas. His more immediate ancestors had been respected for several generations as religious devotees, belonging to the more contemplative variety of that sect known as Sufis—whence perhaps the family name Saffi or Saffavi*—at Ardebil, near the S.E. shore of the Caspian; and the popularity so acquired enabled them to play a part as political adventurers in the scramble which followed the break-up of Timur's Empire, but as adventurers with a religious purpose, appealing to the characteristically Persian sentiment of devotion to the memory of Ali and to the absent twelfth Imám. Ismail Saffavi carried on the same work on a grander scale (1499-1523) and left behind him a kingdom including most of modern Persia and the now Russian province of Georgia, and the fame of having commenced as "king of the Shias," with great spirit and varying success, that essentially religious struggle against the orthodox Ottoman Turks, the masters of Constantinople, and reputed heirs of the Imámate of the Abbasside Caliphs, which has never yet been either decided or appeased, and which was never long suspended until the alarming advance of Russia in the present century began to threaten both combatants with simultaneous extinction.

The Saffavian dynasty has long been extinct, but Persian

* Milton's "Bactrian Sophy," "Paradise Lost," chap. x.

nationality is still identified with the Shia system of religion and law, thereby presenting one of the most formidable obstacles to the political unification of Islam. The differences are in truth numerous and important enough to make it difficult to realise that both systems have ostensibly a common basis in the Korân. So far as the civil law is concerned, this will sufficiently appear in the last chapter of the present work, and in the Digest which is to follow, and the differences in theology, in ritual, and above all in the view taken of Moslem history, are if anything even greater. When Nadir Shah, in furtherance of his schemes of extended empire, insisted that his Persian subjects should cease to call themselves Shias, and sought to reconcile them to the change by obtaining from the Sultan of Turkey the recognition of a fifth orthodox school, to be called the school of Jaafar, and to be on an equality with the schools of Hanífa, Málik, Sháfi, and Hanbal, so that their characteristic institutions might remain unchanged, the compromise wholly failed to conciliate popular sentiment. The sullen submission of the moment was exchanged in a few years for open revolt, and his assassination was the signal for instant return to the old name and the old separateness.

Fixity of the "Sherrah" (Sacred Law) of the Shias.

But although the schism may be for other reasons as incurable as ever, the particular difference to which the term "Shia" owed its original appropriateness practically ceased to exist from the disappearance of the twelfth Imám and the extirpation of the Ismailian "Assassins." At all events the Persian State-religion cannot be contrasted with that of orthodox Turkey on the ground of inculcating devotion to a person in preference to conformity to a set of rules.

Ali is of course held up as the object of unbounded reverence among Shias; but so is Mahomet among the orthodox. Devotion to a dead person, be he Ali or Mahomet, is in practice devotion to a system, if the record of that person's teaching and example has been unalterably fixed, and is only allowed to be explained in the particular way in which the learned of former times have explained it. Now, this appears to be the case with the Shias of Persia no less than with the Sunnís of Turkey. From our point of view, as bearing on the possibilities of innovation in the civil law, the only question is whether there is any living person so far credited with authority to act on behalf of God, Mahomet or Ali (it matters little which), as to be able to take liberties with the Korán and the traditions, or, at least, with the established interpretations thereof. The Persian answer to this question is—pending the second coming of the Mahdi—even more decisively negative than that of Turkish Sunnís; for there is a faint flavour of the Imámate about the Sultan of Turkey, owing to an alleged cession by the last Abbasside Caliph, which is wholly wanting to the quite modern Kajar dynasty of Persia. The only theory of allegiance to which they can appeal is the very simple one which began to commend itself to Moslem thinkers after the break-up of the Bagdad Caliphate, namely, that any ruler in possession should be obeyed so long as he protects the community and pays decent respect to the Sacred Law. It is not to the Shah, but to the trained and certificated interpreters of the Sherrah or Shariat—a different Shariat from that of the Sunnís, but built up on the same Koranic foundation, by similar methods and with analogous though different materials—that the faithful are supposed to look for guidance to their consciences, for determinations of points of law, and in case of need for opinions as to the legality or illegality of the acts of the Shah himself. The most eminent of these "moollahs"* are still dignified with the title "Mujtahíd," which modern Sunnís reserve for the

* The classification of these moollahs, as described by Malcolm, in 1829, seems to be somewhat different from that of the Sunní ulama; their general character more sacerdotal, and their influence with people and sovereign somewhat greater. See Malcolm's "History of Persia," Vol. II., pp. 314-316.

great lawyers of past ages. It is not conferred by the sovereign, but by some informal though apparently unmistakable manifestation of public opinion, which the sovereign finds it his interest to recognise; just as a Mucius Scævola or a Servius Sulpicius would be marked out under the Roman Republic as the leading jurist of the day, whose opinion would be almost certainly accepted by prætors and juries. In this and in other ways the "Sherrah" is pretty effectually secured against modification by the government of the day.

There is indeed, as in other Muhammadan countries, a sort of administrative unwritten law, here called *Urf*, which he declares and administers through officers of his own selection. But in case of conflict between Urf and Sherrah the latter is supposed to prevail, and it is for the Mujtahíds to declare when such conflict has arisen. On the other hand, in Persia, as elsewhere, the odds are tremendously against any sort of reform being initiated or accepted by the ulama themselves as a body. The *à priori* reasons for this, set forth in a preceding chapter, have been strikingly confirmed by recent Persian history.

The Bábís.

The memorable Bábí movement, of which the earlier stages (1850-2) have been admirably portrayed by M. Gobineau, and the later (to 1891) by Mr. E. G. Browne,* found champions and martyrs among some of the most learned and devout of these moollahs, while it elicited from the majority of them a display of ferocious bigotry. Its history illustrates our subject in two ways. It shows that, after three and a half centuries of fixed sacred law, the need

---

* "Les Religions et les Philosophies dans l'Asie Centrale," par le Comte de Gobineau. Paris, 1865. "The Episode of the Bâb," Vol. II. (A Traveller's Narrative), by Edward Granville Browne, M.A., M.B. Cambridge, 1891. Also "A Year amongst the Persians," by the same author, London, 1893.

for reform was felt by the best and most intelligent part of the community to be extreme; and it also tends to show that a reform movement from within, among a community inured to such a system, could only take the form of recognising the supersession of Mahomet's revelation by a new revelation of equal authority adapted to present needs.

CHAPTER IV.

MUHAMMADAN LAW IN INDIA UNDER MUHAMMADAN RULERS.

"When attempts have been made to transplant, without revision, the laws of one country into another, and the consequences of such attempts have proved pernicious, it has been partly, indeed, because the laws were bad *there*, but partly also because they would have been bad anywhere."—BENTHAM.

First Contact with Hindú Idolaters. Death or Tribute?

THE Arab occupation of the border province of Sind (711 A.D.) concerns us only as having raised and settled the question, whether the Hindús ought to be allowed the three-fold option of conversion, death, or tribute, or should be confined to the two former alternatives. The only text of the Korán* which could be quoted as authorising the third course was expressly limited to those "to whom the Scriptures had been given"—a phrase applied by Mahomet to none but Jews and Christians; and it might have been inferred that the text which simply directed the faithful to "strike off the heads of the idolaters,"† etc., was to govern the case of all other infidels.

The question was first raised under the Caliph Omar, in regard to the Fire-worshipping Persians. He was persuaded to admit them to tribute, partly by being reminded of some saying in point attributed to the Prophet himself, and partly by the argument that they also had Scriptures which *they* believed to be divine: an argument which would not help matters much, unless it could be shown that Mahomet himself believed in the divine origin of the Zendavesta.

---

* K. ix. 29. † K. xlvii. 4.

The case of the Hindús was more difficult because, although they also possessed Scriptures, the nature of which may or may not have been known to the Arabs at this date, their whole system of popular worship was unquestionably idolatrous and polytheistic, which that of the Persians was not. The more lenient view was, however, taken by the authorities at Mecca when consulted on the point by the first conqueror of Sind,* and at a somewhat later date the whole matter was put on a broader basis by Abu Hanífa, who held that the stern measures prescribed in the Korán were only directed against the particular form of idolatry carried on at Mecca by Mahomet's own countrymen.

Mahmúd, the Destroyer, and Alberuni, the Inquirer.

The raids of Mahmúd of Ghazni involved the permanent occupation of Lahore, but otherwise can no more be said to have introduced Muhammadan Law into India than those of Julius Cæsar to have introduced Roman Law into Britain. We may, however, note in passing, that while Mahmúd was immortalising himself as the destroyer of idols, a Turkish subject of his, by name Alberuni, was studying sympathetically the religious literature of the Hindús, comparing both their popular mythology and their esoteric philosophy with that of the ancient Greeks, and sensibly pointing out that wholesale plundering and destruction were unpromising instruments of conversion. Unfortunately we hear of very few like him in the period of permanent Muhammadan rule, which commences nearly two centuries later with the "Slave Kings" of Delhi (1206).

Form in which Muhammadan Law was introduced into India.

By this time the progressive period, such as it was, of Muhammadan Law had long come to an end. The period of more or less intelligent condensation and re-arrangement

* Muir's "Caliphate," p. 363.

has just passed its culminating point with the publication of the Hedaya. The Mongol invasions will soon begin and the Caliphate of Bagdad will only drag out half a century more of discreditable existence.

As regards the kind of law which the invaders of Hindústan brought with them, the bulk of them were Turks by race, and as such presumably Sunnís of the Hanáfi school, whose Maulawis would be likely to use the recently-published Hedaya as their chief text-book. But there would doubtless be at all times a fair sprinkling of Persians, who would be more likely than not to favour the Shia doctrines, either openly or secretly, and to avow their opinions more boldly as the sect continued to gain strength in their native country. In fact the example of Shah Ismail Saffavi as the founder of a Shia state was anticipated in one instance, and followed in two others, by adventurers who carved out for themselves kingdoms in the Deccan, and the sect maintained on the whole its ascendancy in that region down to the time of Aurangzíb. On the other hand the Arab traders who settled along the South-western sea-board of India and in the Eastern Archipelago might be expected to carry with them the doctrines of either Málik or Sháfi, and the latter are in fact found to prevail in those parts at the present day.

How did Muhammadan Law affect the Hindús?

However the invaders of India might be scattered, and to whatever school they might belong, pilgrimages to Mecca kept them in touch with the rest of the Moslem world, and a continual influx of fresh recruits helped to keep alive the missionary ardour which other circumstances were constantly tending to cool. The one great peculiarity of their position was the enormous numerical superiority of their unconverted Hindú subjects, a disproportion which showed scarcely any sign of diminution as century after century rolled by. Not only was extermination out of the question, but to keep them in the position assigned by the Shariat to *Zimmís*, or tributary infidels, was by no means easy. The tribute (*jezya*) was sometimes collected, sometimes not. As to how far they were made amenable to, or enjoyed the benefit of, the Muhammadan Civil and Criminal Law, precise information is confessedly not forthcoming, at all events for the pre-Mogul period; but from the continued existence of flourishing schools of Hindú Law all through the Muhammadan period, not by any means exclusively in the still unsubdued Hindú kingdoms, as well as from the careful preservation of old, and very extensive production of new, commentaries (the authors being in some cases known to have held office under Muhammadan rulers), it may be safely inferred that there was plenty of work for Brahman judges to do, and that the threat of excommunication would usually suffice to secure obedience to their decisions within the self-centred caste bodies occupying separate walled-off quarters in the cities, without troubling the Moslem Kázi, while the rural districts, according to Elphinstone, remained to a large extent under the hereditary jurisdiction of Hindú Rajas. Probably no Moslem would ever show his face in such districts, unless with an armed force to extort money.

Disputes between Hindús and Moslems would naturally not turn upon family relations or inheritance, but would arise either out of contracts at the great centres of trade, or out of personal wrongs. These would of course come under the cognizance of Moslem tribunals of some sort; but whether of a Kázi, sworn to administer the Shariat and to ascertain it in case of doubt from a mufti, or of a lay official administering "Urf," and taking his instructions direct from the king, would depend upon circumstances. The general remarks on this subject in Chap. II., p. 2, may be taken as applying with exceptional force to Muhammadan India.

In the department of contract the Hindús had no special reason for clinging to their own usages in preference to the full and clear, if not always very enlightened, precepts of the

Muhammadan Law.* Mr. Baillie thinks that the Muhammadan law of sale regulated the dealings not only of Moslems with Hindús, but of Hindús with each other,† and it is certain that one of its rules at all events, that of pre-emption, governed all sales of land irrespective of the creed of the proprietors. As regards criminal law the Shariat itself made provision for the exemption of *Zimmís* from some of its penal rules (*e.g.*, from the punishment for drinking wine) while expressly declaring them amenable to the others; but as the testimony of an infidel could not be received against a Moslem, the former must always have been at a great disadvantage, whether prosecutor or accused, and must have preferred the irregular jurisdiction of the Amir-i-Adl.‡

Muhammadan Law as applied to Muhammadans.

The strict application of the Shariat, even among the Moslems themselves, must have depended more than elsewhere on the personal disposition of the ruler, because besides the chance of finding support among the more lax of his co-religionists if he chose to snap his fingers at the ulama, there was the further alternative of summoning to his aid the vastly more numerous Hindús. Elphinstone, who admits that we know but little of the internal state of the empire before the accession of Akbar, nevertheless gives us glimpses of Alá-ud-dín Khilji (1295-1316) declaring that "religion had no connection with government, but was the business, or rather the amusement, of private life," and of Firuz Tughlak (1351-1388) prohibiting punishment by mutilation "all the meritoriously because the prohibition was at variance with the Mahometan law." And a footnote

* Except as to lending at interest. This was positively prohibited by the Muhammadan Law, but permitted within certain limits by the Code of Manu.

† The "Moohummadan Law of Sale," by Neil B. E. Baillie, Preliminary Remarks, p. 9.

‡ Imperial Officer of Justice.

by Elphinstone's modern editor directs attention to some remarkable testimony respecting Selim Shah (*alias* Islam Shah), the second of the Affghan princes who kept Humayún out of India for fifteen years, to the effect that he issued "circular orders touching on matters religious, political, or revenue" of so comprehensive and detailed a character as to "obviate the necessity of referring to a Kâzi or Mufti any case relating to matters which had hitherto been settled according to the principles and precepts of Muhammadan Law.*

On the whole it is pretty clear that if the system worked badly in Central Asia, where the Moslems had the field all to themselves, it worked still worse in India, where they were a militant minority, striving vainly to impose it on a thoroughly unsympathetic population. We have therefore the less cause to be surprised that India should have been the scene of perhaps the boldest experiment ever tried by a Moslem sovereign in the way of religious and legal reform.

Akbar.†

I refer to the events which marked the latter half of the reign of Akbar. The first five years of his nominal reign, when he was a minor under the guardianship of Bairam Khan, were rather favourable than otherwise to the ascendancy of the orthodox Ulama, who had good reason according to their own account to rejoice at the collapse of the Affghan dynasty, and who were on the other hand relieved by the death of Humayún, Akbar's father, from grave apprehensions lest he should redeem the pledge given during his exile to the king of Persia by establishing the Shia form of faith as the State religion. We hear in fact of the Kâzis and Muftis pronouncing capital sentences on heretics, with which the young king did not venture to interfere.

* "History of India," pp. 399, 411, 459 note, 482.

† See Blochmann's Ain-i-Akbari, pp. 167-213.

After he had snatched the reins from his guardian at the age of eighteen, there were no doubt several proceedings on his part calculated to cause disquietude in orthodox quarters; the abolition of the jezya;* the employment of Hindús in offices of high trust; then, worse than either, inter-marriage with idolatrous princesses of Rájputána. But the violation of the law of Islam in the last case was disguised, however thinly, by requiring from the Hindú wives a nominal profession of Islam on first entering the harem, and might at all events be regarded as a mere personal irregularity, while the other measures were not without precedent, and might be excused as temporary concessions to political necessity while the fate of the Mogul dynasty still trembled in the balance. The general authority of the sacred law, and of the ulama as its interpreters, remained substantially unimpaired.

Matters began to grow more serious from 1576 or thereabouts, when Akbar's position had been assured by some twenty years of successful warfare, when the conquest of Gujarat had opened out communication with Christian Europe, and when above all his robust intelligence and martial instincts had been brought into contact with the learning and genius of the two sons of Mobarik, Faizi and Abul Fazl. While the former "conducted a systematic inquiry into every branch of the knowledge of the Brahmans," and also undertook to translate the Christian Evangelists; the latter, not less learned but more conversant with affairs of State, engaged his master in a scheme

---

* The Akbarnama positively states this to have been done in the ninth year of his reign, whereas Badaoni refers it to the twenty-fifth. The discrepancy may be explained by supposing that the first abolition was regarded by the orthodox as constitutionally invalid, never having received the sanction of the ulama, and that the edict was promulgated again in a more formal manner after he had been regularly invested with legislative power. See below, p. 80, and compare Elliot's History of India, vol. vi. p. 29, with Blochmann's Ain-i-Akbari, p. 189.

of reform so bold as to throw Al Mámún and the Motazalas altogether into the shade.

First, the influence of the ulama was undermined by means of the famous Thursday evening discussions, so artfully conducted as to split up the orthodox party into enraged factions, besides displaying to the Emperor their common ignorance and intolerance, as also the insecurity of the foundation on which some of the leading rules of the civil law really rested. *E.g.*, on the question (in which Akbar seems to have had a considerable personal stake) as to how many wives a Moslem might lawfully have at the same time, the facts were elicited that one of the ancient Mujtahíds had allowed nine, and another eighteen, on the strength of varying interpretations of the same text of the Korán which as ordinarily construed fixed the limit at four.* And on the closely connected question, whether temporary marriages were legal, the ulama were induced to commit themselves to a collective opinion that not only was the practice sanctioned (as was well known) by the Shia sect, but also (contrary to what had hitherto been supposed) by the orthodox Imám Málik. Whereupon the Emperor (according to our somewhat hostile informant) availing himself of the recognised principle that a Moslem may attach himself to any one of the four orthodox schools at his pleasure, promptly superseded the Chief Kazi, and appointed in his place, for the purpose of determining this question, a Kazi of the Máliki school, who "passed a decree on† the spot declaring *muta* marriages to be legal." We are told, and

* "Marry whatever women ye like by twos, or by threes, or by fours," K. iv. The dissentients read it by "twos *and* threes *and* fours"; $2 + 3 + 4 = 9$; $2 + 2 + 3 + 3 + 4 + 4 = 18$.

† So in Blochmann's translation of Badaoni, Ain-i-Akbari, vol. i, p. 173. Properly speaking, a *decree* is only the final order in a concrete case actually litigated, not an enunciation of an abstract legal proposition, and it would seem from the context that what Akbar really submitted to the new Kazi was his own case, he having contracted many more than four marriages, so that the surplus could only stand, if at all, as *muta* marriages.

can very well believe, that the veteran lawyers "made very long faces" at these proceedings. But much worse was to come.

The same orthodox chronicler to whom we are indebted for our knowledge of these discussions goes on to relate, with increasing disgust, how the Emperor's studies of the early history of Islam inspired him with anything but admiration for the companions of the Prophet, the ultimate sources of the Sunní tradition, and how gradually the discussions began to turn more on the elementary principles of Islam than on isolated points of law, till at last, "as the result of all the influences which were brought to bear on His Majesty, there grew, gradually as the outline on a stone, the conviction in his heart that there were sensible men in all religions, and abstemious thinkers, and men endowed with miraculous powers, among all nations. If some true knowledge were thus everywhere to be found, why should truth be confined to one religion, or to a creed like the Islam, which was comparatively new, and scarcely 1000 years old? Why should one sect assert what another denies, and why should one claim a preference without having the superiority conferred on itself?"

Evidently a new commentary on the Korán, with some attempts to adjust the differences between Málikis and Hanáfis, would not satisfy these new aspirations. To discard the ulama altogether, and to stand forth in his own person as the religious leader of the people, was the course suggested at once by a thoroughly well-grounded consciousness of his own intellectual superiority, and by the practical impossibility of satisfying the orthodox without offending and oppressing the bulk of his subjects. The revolution was, however, carried out as far as possible by constitutional methods. In September, 1579 A.D., the signatures were obtained, by some means or other, of the two rival orthodox leaders, of the chief Kázi and the chief Mufti of the Empire, and of two other learned persons, to the following very remarkable document.

"Whereas Hindustân has now become the centre of security and peace, and the land of justice and beneficence, a large number of people, especially learned men and lawyers, have immigrated and chosen this country for their home, Now we, the principal Ulamas, who are not only well versed in the several departments of law and in the principles of jurisprudence, and well acquainted with the edicts which rest on reason or testimony, but are also known for our piety and honest intentions, have duly considered the deep meaning, *first*, of the verse of the Korân (Sur. iv. 62) "Obey God, and obey the Prophet, and those who have authority among you," and *secondly*, of the genuine (?) tradition:—"Surely the man who is dearest to God on the day of judgment is the Amír-i-Adil, whosoever obeys the Amir obeys Me; and whosoever rebels against the Amír rebels against Me; and thirdly, of several other proofs based on reasoning or testimony; and we have agreed that the rank of a Sultan-i-Adil (a just ruler) is higher in the eyes of God than the rank of a Mujtahíd. Further, we declare that the King of the Islam, Amir of the Faithful, shadow of God in the world, Abul Fath Jálaluddin Muhammad Akbar Padishah-i-Ghazi, whose kingdom God perpetuate, is a most just, a most wise, and a most God-fearing king.

"Should, therefore, in future, a religious question come up, regarding which the opinions of the Mujtahíds are at variance, and His Majesty, in his penetrating understanding and clear wisdom, be inclined to adopt, for the benefit of the nation and as a political expedient, any of the conflicting opinions which exist on that point, and issue a decree to that effect, we do hereby agree that such a decree shall be binding on us and on the whole nation.

"Further, we declare that, should His Majesty think fit to issue a new order, we and the nation shall likewise be bound by it, provided always that such order be not only in accordance with some verse of the Korán, but also of real benefit to the nation; and further that any opposition on the part of the subjects to such an order as passed by His Majesty shall involve damnation in the world to come, and loss of religion and property in this life.

"This document has been written with honest intentions, for the glory of God, and the propagation of Islam, and is signed by us, the principal Ulama and lawyers, in the month of Rajab of the year 987 of the Hijra* (= 1579 A.D.)"

Though the authority hereby conferred on the Emperor was limited in terms to deciding questions as to which the Mujtahíds might be at variance, and to the promulgation of orders in accordance with some verse of the Korán, even these restraints could be safely disregarded, so soon as the body of the ulama, which had professed to impose them, had been broken up and dispersed, a measure which was very soon carried out. The two leaders were recommended to go on a pilgrimage to Mecca, while the chief Kazi and others were sent to occupy subordinate posts in distant provinces, and the Chief Mufti declared himself a convert to the new religion now publicly proclaimed as Dín-i-Iláhí, or the Divine Faith.

The bearing of this revolution upon our subject consists in this, that it confirmed the legal changes already made and facilitated other changes in real or supposed contravention of the Shariat. Among the latter were:—

1. Prohibition of marriages between first cousins, which the Korán permitted. This was an approximation to Hindú principles, and as such might help to mitigate the aversion with which the votaries of each religion regarded the practices of the other. It may also have been intended to protect a girl against an abuse of power on the part of a male paternal cousin who might as such be her guardian,

* As to the mode of reducing dates A.H. to datos A.D., see chap. i. p 10. The abolition of this very inconvenient lunar year was one of Akbar's reforms, which remained in force down to the reign of Aurangzíb.

and might dispose of her in marriage to himself, instead of negotiating for her a more advantageous match.*

2. Express permission of wine-drinking under medical advice and Government regulation.

3. Polygamy prohibited, except in case of the first wife's barrenness. This again was in accordance with Manu's counsels of perfection, if not with Hindú Law as actually enforced. Akbar's conversion to this view must have been a surprise to his courtiers, if the account above quoted of his share in the Thursday discussions is accurate; and from the silence of history it may be safely inferred that he was not so quixotically and cruelly consistent as to divorce his own supernumerary wives.

6. Every *man* to be at liberty to change his religion if he thought fit; thus reversing the rule of Muhammadan Law, that a male apostate should be punished with death. The new rule did not apply to *women*, who were to be forced back, whether Hindús or Muhammadans, to the religion of their husbands or fathers.

7. Disputes between Hindús to be decided by learned Brahmans and not by Muhammedan Kazis. This is mentioned by Badáoni as an innovation, but the novelty, if any, can have been only in the formal recognition of existing usage.

The balance was kept even by other enactments directed against some of the worst practices connected with the Hindú religion.

Intrinsically valuable as these reforms were, they would have been much too dearly purchased, like those of Mahomet, at the cost of admitting the pretensions of a new Prophet. But happily Akbar made no such pretensions.† While

* See below, chap. vi.

† If any such pretensions were made for him, it was not in such a way as to imply infallibility, and they were very speedily dropped. See some remarks on this subject in an article of mine in the *Indian Magazine*, for February, 1894, "Akbar, the Great Mogul," ii.

striking off old fetters he forged no new ones for posterity. His new religion was merely the eclectic result of his own honest inquiries and varied experiences, put into shape by the philosophic genius of his friend Abul Fazl, and commended to his other friends for what in their judgment it might be worth. So far from enforcing new dogmas on the people at large, he continued to employ in high office both Moslems and Hindús who positively refused to become members of the "Divine Faith." His religion was negatively connected with his legislation, in that it relieved his conscience from Islamic restraints. Instead of building up a temporal sovereignty on a basis of supernatural claims, he ran considerable risk of weakening, by his frank avowal of heterodoxy, the fabric of power which he had built up by twenty years of valour and statesmanship.

Partial Reaction under Jahangir and Shah Jahán.

Akbar's new religion died with him, if not before him. Its real inventor, Abul Fazl, was waylaid and slain by a Hindú raja, and Akbar's own son and destined successor boasted after his father's death of having instigated the murder.

It is probably untrue that "he died in all the forms of a good Mussulman,"* but it is a fair inference from the currency of such a story that he did not in any way encourage the continuance of organised opposition to Islam. In truth it was quite in the spirit of his religion, a favourite watchword of which was "peace with all," that his last moments should be spent in efforts of reconciliation, rather than in emphasising the peculiarities of a creed which so few were capable of appreciating. †

---

* See the Editor's footnote to Elphinstone's "History of India," p. 531.

† If he made any speech at all on his deathbed; but the whole account o the scene comes from a very suspicious source, namely Jehangir himself, and I am inclined to disbelieve it.

From the accession of this Salím, thenceforth known as Jahangír, Islam became again the established religion; but it does not follow that the practice of the tribunals was at once brought back to the standard of the Shariat. That a good many of Akbar's heretical ordinances remained in force all through the reign of his successor, is clear from the fact that Jahangír's successor, Shah Jahán, is credited by Mussulman historians with "having directed his imperial care to the re-introduction of the customs of Islam, the strict observance of which had died away, and turned his august zeal to rebuilding the edifice of the law of the Prophet, which had all but decayed."* And it would appear that even the zeal of Shah Jahán left a good deal to be done by his successor in order to bring Muhammadan India into full conformity with the orthodox standard. It was only in the third year of Aurangzíb (A.D. 1659) that the lunar era of the Hijra was restored as above mentioned; soon afterwards all taxes not authorised by the Shariat were remitted, and at last, in 1676, the obnoxious *jezya* was re-imposed.†

The Fatáwa Alamgíri of Aurangzíb.

In the meantime great efforts had been made to revive the study of the Shariat, and India beheld, for the first and last time, a really important work on Muhammadan Law published by a Muhammadan sovereign. It is in fact referred to outside India as the Fatáwa-i-Hind, *i.e.*, the Indian collection of precedents, but in India as the Fatáwa Alamgírí, from the Emperor's title Alamgír, "Lord of the World." It is a methodical and annotated compilation of *fatwas*, judicial opinions of the mujtahíds of the best period: corresponding, therefore, so far, to the Digest of Justinian, but differing in the very important point that it does not profess to derive any of its binding force from the Emperor who ordered its publication, or to supersede the

* Blochmann's "Ain-i-Akbari," vol. i., p. 213.

† Elphinstone's "India," p. 636.

original sources from which its matter was extracted. It was commenced about 1670 A.D., the funds for it being provided by discontinuing the allowance hitherto given to the Court historian for compiling the annals of the reign.* The work itself was of course in Arabic, still the recognised vehicle of religious instruction, and the language in which the decisions cited were originally delivered, but (like the Latin of Justinian's Digest) a foreign tongue to the bulk of those for whose use it was intended. It was therefore translated into Persian by the Emperor's daughter: a striking proof of his earnest desire to make it practically useful.

The complete Reaction under Aurangzíb and its Lessons.

Akbar and Aurangzíb are beyond compare the two most thoughtful and consistent statesmen in the long series of Mogul Emperors, and they represent the opposite poles of Mogul policy in relation to Muhammadan Law.

The former was resolved to be a just ruler first, a devout Moslem if possible afterwards, and as experience convinced him that the two things were incompatible he gradually ceased to be a Moslem at all.

The latter was also a lover of justice, but his sole standard of justice, from which he would not willingly depart a hair's breadth, was the law of Islam.

Akbar is naturally preferred, both as a man and as a statesman, by European historians, and the feeling that it is the special mission of the British Government to revive his policy and fulfil his aspirations has received a kind of national consecration from one of the last poems of our late Laureate. Aurangzíb is no less decidedly the favourite of Muhammadan writers, and his claims to their regard, as the "Puritan King of India," who "left nothing undone of the whole duty of the Muslim," have been effectively set forth by Mr. Stanley Lane-Poole, in one of the most interesting

* See Baillie on the "Moohummadan Law of Sale," preliminary remarks.

of the "Rulers of India" series. To them the argument from results is of course not conclusive; but they themselves admit that so far as it goes it is against them, and the only effect of rendering fuller justice to the ability and devotion of their champion is to bring out still more clearly the utter hopelessness of his task. The broad facts of the case are that whereas Akbar, dying at the age of sixty-three, after a reign of forty-nine years marked by steadily widening sympathies towards non-Muhammadan persons and institutions, left a vast and well-knit empire where he had found chaos; Aurangzíb, dying at the age of ninety, after a reign of fifty years devoted to Moslem ascendancy and the enforcement of the whole law of Islam, left a disorganised administration, a bankrupt treasury, his main army in full retreat before the infidels, once loyal feudatories disaffected, and much worse things to come which he did not live to see.

The primary cause of failure was of course the fact that the system of law and religion which he deemed it his duty to enforce was odious in all its forms to seven-eighths of the population, while his particular form of it (the Sunní) was detested by a powerful minority of the remaining eighth. But we are thus thrown back on the inquiry, why the system had failed to commend itself, after an acquaintance of five or six centuries, to a people so submissive and so receptive as the Hindús, and in competition with institutions so difficult to defend as the Brahminical—an inquiry which can only be answered generally in the words of Bentham, as prefixed to this chapter.

The laws of Islam, taken in the lump, the only way in which their alleged sacred origin allowed them to be taken, and chiefly because they could only be so taken, were bad anywhere and for any community, and became worse and worse the further they were transplanted from their original surroundings: worse under the Caliphate of Bagdad than at Medina under the "rightly-directed"

Caliphs, and worse for Hindús of the seventeenth century than for Bagdad in the ninth.

Within half a century from the death of Aurangzíb, fully half India was either directly subject, or tributary to Hindú Governments; and the battle of Pánipat (A.D. 1760) proved even more decisively the inability of the indigenous Moslems to retain their hold over the remainder without foreign aid, than it proved the inability of the Hindús to secure the triumph of Brahminism so long as the highlands continued to roll down fresh torrents of Moslem invasions. But the way through the Khaibar Pass was at last closed by a power which was neither Hindú nor Moslem, and by that time the second-rate Muḥammadan states built up out of the débris of Aurangzíb's empire were maintaining a precarious existence by means of alliance with the East India Company, under whose direct rule no inconsiderable number of Muhammadans had already passed. Here, therefore, the interest shifts to the great experiment of working Muhammadan laws under a Christian Government, which must form the subject of our next chapter.

CHAPTER V.

HISTORY AND PRESENT FOOTING OF ANGLO-MUHAMMADAN LAW.

"Me, too, the black-winged Azrael overcame,
But Death had ears and eyes; I watched my son,
And those that followed, loosen, stone from stone,
All my fair work; and from the ruin arose
The shriek and curse of trampled millions, even
As in the time before; but while I groaned,
From out the sunset poured an alien race,
Who fitted stone to stone again, and Truth,
Peace, Love, and Justice came and dwelt therein."

TENNYSON'S *Akbar's Dream.*

WHATEVER the late Laureate may have meant to indicate by the verses above quoted, it is unfortunately the fact that Akbar's dream remains a dream still, with just such small foretaste of realisation as may encourage perseverance on the lines already marked out for us. The present chapter will disclose, to some extent, the evidence for this assertion in relation to one subordinate, but not unimportant, department of British administration, which the spirit of Akbar may be supposed to contemplate with rather special interest.

The East India Company as deputy of the Mogul.

In 1765, Shah Alum, the titular Emperor of Hindustán, found himself for the second time a prisoner of the English, who had been for eight years past in military occupation of his provinces of Bengal and Bahar, setting up one puppet after another as nominal governor (*subahdar*); and who had lately proceeded further to take possession of Oudh, after defeating the combined forces of His Imperial Majesty and of the local Governor. Though his capital was in hands supposed to be friendly, he dared not present himself there unless he could induce a European force to accompany him, while a great part of his hereditary Empire was exchanging the law of the Korán for the law of the Shasters under the rule of the Marathas. Under these circumstances it cost him little to agree to the terms proposed by Clive, and to execute the *farmán*, with which the history of Anglo-Indian (including Anglo-Muhammadan) law practically begins.

Its purport was to split up the powers previously exercised by the subahdar of Bengal over the the three provinces of Bengal proper, Bahar, and Orissa, into two portions. One portion was granted to the East India Company's nominee and puppet, under the title of Nawáb Nazím; the remainder, under the name of Diwaní, was conferred on the Company itself.

The office of Diwán was generally understood to include: (1) the right of collecting taxes, and generally the management of the finances; and (2) the right and duty of superintending the administration of *civil* justice. The Nizámat included the supervision of criminal law and police, and would have included the military department, but for the fact that the Company allowed no military force but their own to exist. It has been said* that this *farmán* contained a clause binding the Company "to use their best endeavours in deciding causes, and settling matters agreeably to the rules of Moohumud, and the laws of the Empire;" but whether this was so or not, they did not for several years use any endeavours at all, nor trouble themselves to inquire how causes were decided in their new territories. They

* By Mr. Baillie, in his work on the Muhammadan Contract of Sale, preliminary remarks, p. 12, note. But no such clause appears in Aitchison's Treaties. The existence of a similar clause in a still earlier *farman* is asserted in a speech of Sir J. Elliot on the impeachment of Impey, as cited in Sir J. Stephen's Nuncomar and Impey, vol. 2, p. 26.

simply appointed one native, a Muhammadan, to exercise both the administrative functions properly belonging to the Company and those nominally reserved to the Nawáb Nazím in Bengal proper, and another native, who happened to be a Hindú, to exercise similar functions in Bahar. (Orissa, the third province included in the subah, was at this time in the power of the Maráthas.) They looked to these two men to raise the revenue, and to hand over the surplus thereof to the Company, leaving them in other respects a perfectly free hand.

After five or six years the Directors awoke to the fact that as the result of this system there were no surplus revenues to be handed over, but, on the contrary, a grave and increasing deficit, together with increasing distress among the people, about a third of whom were carried off by famine in 1770. Then they sent out Warren Hastings, as the ablest of their servants, to see how a better financial result could be brought about, expressly instructing him to depose the two provincial Governors, and to "cause the Company to stand forth as Diwán."

The Bengal Regulations of 1772.

Hastings saw clearly that at any rate one indispensable step to the realisation of profit for the Company was to afford some measure of security to the taxpayers. The result of the inquiries into the existing arrangements was that, while ten different kinds of judicial authorities were concentrated at Murshidábád, the capital of the Subah, elsewhere "the regular course of justice was everywhere suspended, but everyone exercised it who had the power of compelling others to submit to his decisions." His first attempt to remedy this state of things was embodied in the Regulations of August 15, 1772, thus described by Mr. Field :—

* "Two Courts, a Diwání, or Civil Court, and a Faujdari, or

* "Regulations of the Bengal Code," p. 136.

Criminal Court, were instituted for each provincial division or "Collectorship" as then constituted. The Collector, on the part of the Company as Diwán, presided over the Diwáni Adálat or Civil Court, which had jurisdiction in all disputes concerning property, real or personal, and all cases of debt, disputed accounts, contracts, partnerships, and demands of rent. The Kazi and Mufti of the district and two Mulvís sat in the Faujdari Adálat to expound the Mahomedan Law and determine how far accused persons were guilty of its violation; but it was made the Collector's duty to see that the proceedings were regular, and the decisions fair and impartial. An appeal lay from these courts to the Sadr Diwání Adálat, or Chief Civil Court, and to the Nizámat, or Chief Criminal Court, respectively. The Sadr Diwání Adálat consisted of the President and Members of Council, assisted by the Native Officers of the Khalsa, or Exchequer. The Nizámat Adálat consisted of the Chief Officer of Justice appointed on the part of the Nawáb Nazím and styled the Darogah-i-Adálat, the Head Kazi and Mufti, and three eminent Mulvís. It was their duty to revise the proceedings of the Faujdari Adálat, and in capital cases to prepare the sentence for the warrant of the Nazím."

As regards the substantive law to be administered in the Diwání Adálat, the Regulations enjoined that—

"In all suits regarding inheritance, marriage, caste, and other religious usages or institutions, the laws of the Korán with respect to Mahomedans, and those of the Shasters with respect to Gentús,* are to be invariably adhered to; and on such occasions the Mulvís and Brahmans are to attend and expound the law."

Note particularly the word "other" in this clause, showing a clear perception of the fact that marriage, inheritance,

* "A term borrowed from the Portuguese to designate those who are now called Hindús. It properly means Gentiles or heathen." Wilson's "Glossary."

etc., were religious institutions of the Muhammadans and Hindús in the sense that the laws governing them were to be gathered from their respective Scriptures, not from the ordinances of any secular government; in short that each of the rival systems of religion included a system of civil law, any attempt to modify which would expose the government to the risks inseparable from conflicts with highly-organised religious bodies.

And inasmuch as the policy of Hastings was certainly to disturb existing usage as little as possible, the provision for Brahmans as well as for Mulvís goes to prove that the practice of referring purely Hindú disputes to Hindú pundits, formally enjoined by Akbar, and probably observed long before his time, had maintained itself in spite of Aurangzíb, or had been restored after his death at least in the Eastern provinces. It may with equal certainty be inferred from the preceding regulation respecting the Faujdari Adálat, that in criminal cases it had not been the practice to take account of any Scriptural law except the Muhammadan—perhaps not very much of that.

In 1774 the functions of the collectors in connection with the Diwáni Adálat were transferred to six so-called "Provincial Councils of Revenue," thus concentrating in fewer centres the slender stock of judicial ability which the Company could command. Whether or not the change was an improvement, it did not save the system from the unqualified, and not wholly undeserved, contempt of the first set of trained English lawyers who were brought into contact with it.

The Supreme Court.

The first collision between Oriental laxity and English judicial pedantry, so disastrous to the parties immediately concerned, so curious and instructive to the student of legal history, was brought about in this wise. In 1773 a "Supreme Court" was constituted by Act of Parliament and Royal Charter, with civil jurisdiction over all persons in Calcutta,* and over all persons in the service of the East India Company throughout the new territories. Sir Elijah Impey came out as Chief Justice in 1774, and in 1777 occurred the famous Patna case, which afterwards figured as one of the grounds of his impeachment, and which is worth narrating here on account of its bearing on the early history of Anglo-Muhammadan law.

The Patna Case.†

Shahbaz Beg, a native of Cabul, came to India as a soldier of fortune, served with credit under the East India Company, and thereby amassed considerable property, with which he settled at Patna, and married a wife, Naderah Begum, by whom, however he had no issue. So far as

---

* Calcutta was, in a legal sense, a purely English town, and had never been anything else. It had grown up round the English factory which had never acknowledged any law but the English, even while the territorial sovereignty of the Mogul Emperors was undisputed. Of the native inhabitants it could be said with truth that the English law had not been obtruded on them, but that they had come to it, and that if they disliked it they had only to cross a ditch. (See Sir E. Impey's speech in bar of impeachment, pp. 32-34.) So far, the Act was merely confirmatory of the existing state of things. On the other hand, the newly-acquired territories would not, even if directly annexed to the British Crown, have come *ipso facto* under English law, the general presumption being that the laws of a ceded province remain as they were until expressly altered. Still less could the mere fact that certain British subjects having large powers delegated to them by the native rulers justify the exercise of jurisdiction over the native subjects of the latter under patent from the King of Great Britain.

† The chief source of information as to this case is the "Patna Appendix" to the report of the House of Commons Committee on the petition of Touchet and others, inhabitants of Calcutta, complaining of the Supreme Court, in the Record Department of the India Office. I was directed to it by the references in Sir J. F. Stephen's "Nuncomar and Impey," vol. ii., chap. 12; but careful study of its contents has led me to conclusions which differ very considerably from those of the learned judge. One cause of divergence is that he appears to me to have almost entirely overlooked the important bearing of Muhammadan law upon the case.

appears, his nearest relative was one Allum Beg, his brother by the mother's side, and also his paternal first cousin, who at his invitation came from Cabul to visit him, bringing with him one of his four sons, by name Behader Beg. Allum Beg himself soon returned to Cabul, but by arrangement between the brothers, Behader Beg remained with his uncle, married the daughter of the latter's wife's sister, and was led to expect that ultimately, when he had gained sufficient experience, Shahbaz Beg would hand over to him his Indian property and himself return to end his days in his native country, where also he had some property. But in 1776, before this plan had been carried out, Shahbaz Beg died, and a struggle for the property soon commenced between the widow and the nephew. As is usual in India, the jewels and other valuables belonging to the deceased, as also the slave women, was kept in the women's apartments, and to that extent the widow had the advantage of possession, though as regards the house generally one was as much in possession as the other. Behader Beg therefore made the first move by presenting to the three or four Englishmen who constituted the Provincial Council of Patna a petition in Persian, which, as entered in English on their minutes, runs as follows :—*

"Mirza Shahbaz Beg Khan sent for me from Cabool, and thus addressed me :—"You are my brother's son, and as such now in the place of my own son; I have made you master of my effects, and when you have sufficient knowledge and experience I shall deliver over to you the charge of everything, and go myself to Cabool." It is known to the English gentlemen and to everyone, that he established me as his son and heir,† and I accordingly received a Khelaut (complimentary present) from the Governor-General. Now

* A more full and literal translation, made for the purpose of the subsequent civil suit, is given in the "Patna Appendix," No. 1.

† "His heir, and the representative of himself," in the fuller translation

the wife of the late Khan being instigated by interested people, has removed and secreted the effects. I request, therefore, that you will furnish me with a few Hircarrahs (constables) to prevent the removal of the goods, and to cause such as have been carried away to be brought back, and that you will give directions to the Cauzee (Kazi) to ascertain my right and acquaint you therewith."

By the Regulations of 1772 the duty of the Provincial Council, as representing the Diwáni Adálat, was to summon the widow before them and try the case themselves, calling some Mulví to their assistance for the purpose of expounding the law. Strictly speaking there was no room for the intervention of a Kazi, as distinguished from a Mulvi or Mufti, inasmuch as the civil jurisdiction properly belonging to the former, according to Muhammadan law, had been transferred to the Council; but the petition itself shows that the practice had been otherwise. In point of fact the European civil servants of the Company, conscious of their ignorance and pre-occupied with the (to them) much more interesting revenue business, had maintained the native judicature just as they found it, only treating what would formerly have been the final decision as a report to themselves, which they might or might not think fit to confirm.* There was a Kazi for the province of Bahar, who had held that office for some years before 1772, under an appointment from Shah Alum, the Mogul Emperor, apparently based in some way on the recommendation of other learned men of the province. In that capacity he constituted, with the chief Mufti, the Faujdari or criminal court; and he had also been appointed to be the chief law-officer attached to the Diwáni Adálat, by the English Chief of that body, at a salary of £120 per

* Even this reservation was obscured from the view of the Supreme Court by the mistake of the official translator in rendering "fatwa" by "decree," thereby enabling the Chief Justice to assert with some plausibility that the Patna Council treated the report of their law officers as the decree and their own order as the award of execution.

annum,* which the regulations forbade him to supplement by fees of any kind. He was only removable by the principal Kazi of the Subah, resident at Murshídabád, who could no doubt be compelled by some means or other to give effect to the wishes of the Company; but in both cases the popular respect for their person and office was so essential a condition of their usefulness that any arbitrary displacement, or any open treatment of them as mere servants of the Company, would have been highly impolitic. The same remarks would apply generally to the three provincial Muftís, except that their functions were, even from the Muhammadan point of view, merely consultative, and that their stipends were naturally smaller. One of them stated afterwards that he had been receiving 24 rupees a month (= £28 16s. a year) from the Government, but that fees for registering documents of various kinds made up his income to 150 rupees a month.†

Treatment of the case by the Company's Judges and their Muhammadan Assistants.

Under these circumstances it is easy to understand, if not altogether to justify, the action of the Council in remitting the whole investigation to the Kazi and Muftís in the first instance, without distinguishing questions of law from questions of fact, and from purely executive functions, and still more easy both to understand and to justify the conduct of those officers in accepting the commission.

* Sir James Stephen has pointed out that this would be about $\frac{1}{67}$th of the salary of the Chief Justice of the Supreme Court; but the inference (coarsely insinuated by Impey) that the Kazi was proportionately more likely than himself to be corrupt and incompetent, falls to the ground when we remember that the office was a sacred one in the eyes of his co-religionists, whose reverence for the holder thereof would probably be in inverse ratio to his display of wealth.

† In his case, also, the taking of fees was forbidden by the letter of the Regulation, but it would be a poor compliment to the intelligence of Hastings to suppose that he meant the restriction to be enforced where the Government pay was below that of an English day-labourer.

The Order of the Council, entered in English on the minutes, reached the law officers in the shape of a Persian "*perwannah*" of slightly different purport, directing them in effect:—

(1) to take an inventory of the property of the deceased, in presence of both disputants;

(2) to collect the money and goods, seal them up, and provide for their safe custody;

(3) to report to the Council as to the rights of the parties; 'that according to ascertained facts and legal justice you transmit to the Council a written report on this cause under your seals, specifying how much is to be given, to what persons, according to the Koran and the decrees.'*

All three branches of this commission were within the proper province of the Kazi according to Muhammadan Law, though only the last, and that only partially, had been assigned to the law-officers under Hastings' regulations.

After an interval of about three weeks the Kazi and Muftís reported in effect as follows. (Jan. 27, 1777.)

Behader Beg had claimed the whole inheritance as nephew and adopted son of the deceased, alleging in support of the latter claim merely the facts already stated in his petition. The widow had also put forward through Kojah Zekeriah, sister's son of the deceased, a claim to the whole inheritance based on three distinct documents:—(1) a *Mohurnama, i.e.*, a deed of dower, or marriage settlement; (2) a *Hibanama*, or deed of transfer, wrongly rendered "will" in the English translation presented to the Council, as was afterwards admitted; (3) an "*Ekraraum*' (Ikrar-i-am) or acknowledgment.

As to the *Mohurnama*, they had only to report that the widow's agent failed to produce it and at last said it had been mislaid. There was nothing therefore to disprove the assertion of Behader Beg, that the sum named in it was only

* *i.e.*, *fatwas*, the responses of ancient jurists, such as Abu Hanífa, Abu Yúsuf, etc.

1,200 Rs., which had all been paid by the deceased in his lifetime. As to the other two deeds, the law-officers were of opinion that "they were not deserving of credit and from many circumstances bore the marks of being spurious" (or according to another translation "were suspicious and invalid") and that the second would not in any case establish the widow's right of succession, and they concluded "as in short everything urged on the part of Kojah Zekeriah seems to want support, and as the order of succession * given by Behader Beg appears clear and explicit, we would recommend that, except the *ultumghaw*, which does not compose a part of the inheritance, all the deceased's property be divided into four shares, whereof three should be given (in charge) to Behader Khan, his father being the legal heir of the deceased, and himself the adopted son; and the remaining one to Nadera, the deceased's widow."

The point of chief importance to us in this Report is to see how far it faithfully represents the Muhammadan Law bearing on the case.

In the first place it is clear law that the only widow of a childless Moslem dying intestate is entitled to one-fourth of his net assets, after payment of his debts and funeral expenses. It very frequently happens that she has a prior claim to something on account of "deferred dower," in respect of which she is on the same footing as any other creditor, and our Courts have since held that she may retain any property of her husband which happens to be in her possession until this claim is satisfied. Sometimes, indeed, the unpaid dower is so large as to leave little or nothing for claimants by inheritance. The law-officers were therefore quite right in directing their attention first of all

* "Story" in the translation supplied to the Supreme Court, thus giving rise to Impey's unfounded sneer that the law-officers considered a story to be proved if it were well told. The matters of pedigree referred to, and the treatment of Behader by his uncle, were never really disputed.

to the *mohurnama*, and in considering that its non-production told strongly against the widow.

As to the other deeds, they ought to have declared more explicitly that, forgery or no forgery, such documents could not possibly stand in law; and that, if the deceased did really execute them in his lifetime, it must have been because he did not properly know what he was about.* A Moslem in good health may no doubt dispose of his property to any one he pleases, but only on condition of actually delivering it then and there to the grantee. Now this *Hibanama* purported to be a declaration on the part of Shahbaz Beg that he had actually delivered into his wife's possession not only all his property of whatever kind at Patna, but also all his present and future property in Cabul; and then went on to stipulate that maintenance should be provided thereout for his sister's son, Kojah Zekeriah, and 500 Rs. per annum should be paid to Behader, on condition of service and obedience. The second deed, called *Ekraraum*, bearing date the day after that of the first, purported to be a declaration by Shahbaz Beg that whatever property was then in his possession belonged legally to his wife, and was held by him as a loan (*ariat*) from her, thus making it absolutely clear that the transfer of possession asserted in the first deed was a mere pretence; and that the object of the whole transaction, if it ever really took place, must have been to evade the rigorous limitations which Muhammadan Law imposes on the testamentary power.† Even on the supposition, which was opposed to all the known facts, that he had suddenly resolved to violate the understanding on which his brother's son had been entrusted to his charge

* According to one translation of the Report they did not positively assert that the deeds were forged, but only that they were "suspicious and invalid" which would certainly have been the safest line to take.

† As to these, see the next chapter; and compare Maine's "Ancient Law," chap. vi., pp. 203-205, as to the success of the corresponding fiction in the history of the Roman will.

and to leave everything to his childless wife, the law would not allow him to do this by will or deathbed gift, or by any process except that which King Lear adopted to his cost in providing for his daughters.

Putting these deeds out of the question, they were certainly right in declaring that of all the persons whose names were before them Allum Beg had the best claim to the remaining three-fourths according to the rules of inheritance. The official translation, "legal heir," does less than justice to their accuracy; for it seems that they really applied to him the two expressions *saheb farz* and *asba* (ásabah); in the language of Anglo-Muhammadan Law, "Sharer" and "Residuary." As half-brother by the mother's side he was entitled to a one-sixth "share"; as paternal cousin he was entitled, failing nearer agnates, to the residue.

They were also probably right, under all the circumstances of the case, in allowing Behader Beg to take charge of his father's share. To retain it under lock and key until the latter could be communicated with would have been extremely inconvenient, and there was fair evidence that both Allum Beg and the deceased had been on the best of terms with Behader, and had really intended to place him as nearly as possible in the position of son to his uncle, and to make him the head of the Patna branch of the family. This was probably all they meant when they spoke of him as the deceased's "adopted son"; for if they had really regarded him as entitled by virtue of adoption to inherit like a real son—which would have been a gross blunder in law—they would have assigned to the widow not one-fourth, but one-eighth.*

Lastly as to the "*ultumghaw*" (altamgha). This was a

* See the next chapter. It may be added that adoption in the Roman or Hindú sense is as unknown to English as to Muhammadan Law, so that the English gentlemen would not be likely to understand anything more by it than is above expressed.

grant of rent-free land which was in form merely personal, not hereditary; and it was outside the province of the law-officers to take notice of a custom to re-grant it to some member of the first grantee's family.

On the whole, they seem to have discharged very fairly the only function properly belonging to them under the Regulations. They could hardly be expected to acquit themselves with equal credit as a tribunal for trying questions of fact, the task irregularly forced upon them by the Council. Certainly, as regards the only question of fact which was seriously contested, viz., the genuineness of the deeds produced on behalf of the widow, their efforts to ascertain the truth were feeble, and their reasoning inconclusive; but it was probably impossible for them to do better without powers and appliances which they do not appear to have possessed; nor was it really necessary for the purpose of their report to decide positively whether the deeds were forged or not. The burden of proof was on the widow, and they had ample grounds for affirming that she had wholly failed to prove the only facts which, by law, could interfere with the division of the property according to the ordinary rules of inheritance. They were also fully justified in intimating, on a mere inspection of the documents submitted to them, so much suspicion of foul play in some shape, forgery, fraud, or undue influence, as would naturally lead to further inquiry, and, possibly, to a criminal prosecution.

The order of the Provincial Council, based on this report, was so worded as to make it quite clear that Behader Beg was only to have the three-fourths as representing his father, and not as representing the deceased; and it also dealt with the "ultumghaw," but in other respects it confirmed the report, and directed the Kazi and Muftís to carry out the division. It seems, however, that the members had themselves no very clear notion of what they had decided, for their chief afterwards reported to the Governor-General that the widow's claim was based on a *will*, which was found to be forged, and that Behader Beg was to have the property on the ground of consanguinity to the deceased, *and also on the ground of the latter having appointed him his heir;* whereas another member afterwards deposed that he considered the decision to have been in favour of the father, Allum Beg. Hastings' reply betrays, incidentally, that he had no more understanding than his subordinates of the points of law involved; but he remarked on the irregularity of deputing the law-officers to try questions of fact, at the same time that he confirmed, from his own recollection, the fact of Behader Beg having been introduced to him by Shahbaz as his destined heir.

The difficulties experienced in overcoming the passive resistance of the widow to the carrying out of the division illustrate Indian usage and the purdah system rather than true Muhammadan Law, and the proceedings, which finally brought matters to a crisis, were taken by the Council through their own servants, and not by the law-officers. Muhammadan Law, of the Hanáfi sort at all events, would not support Behader Beg's claim to have the guardianship of her person as the nearest available male paternal kinsman of her husband; nor his plea, that her husband's family would be disgraced if she were simply allowed to go where she pleased with her legal share of the property; but custom was probably on his side.* Practically, some male relative must take charge of her until she married again, and the real question was, whether it should be Behader Beg, her husband's brother's son, or Kojah Zekeriah, her husband's sister's son, or one of her blood relations. Matters had been further complicated by the hasty action of the Council in arresting Kojah Zekeriah and some others on a charge of forgery, and committing them for trial to the supreme native

* The draft penal code of Hyderabad, framed for a Muhammadan State, but not rigidly conforming to the Korán, treats an adult woman as under the guardianship of her husband while he lives, and of her sons after her death. See below, p. 115.

Criminal Court at Murshídabád,* so that there was no one who could be trusted to receive, on her behalf, the share of the realised assets which had been set apart for her. On the other hand, she baffled the law officers and Council for some time by refusing to live in the house now that Behader was in possession of it, and withdrawing with the slave-women and other effects (including that dangerous implement, her husband's seal), to a sort of sanctuary, into which they long scrupled to intrude. At last, apparently on the suggestion of Hastings himself, the clumsy expedient of isolating her and trying to starve her into submission was abandoned, and a batch of female constables was employed to take from her by force whatever was supposed to belong to the inheritance.

The widow's remedy—if she considered herself to be aggrieved—was, according to the regulations, an appeal to the Governor-General and the Council, assisted by the chief Kazi and Muftís, as Sadr Diwáni Adálat. She did, in fact, send two written petitions to Hastings, but the only action he took thereon was to write privately to the chief of the Patna Council for explanations. Possibly a formal appeal might at some time or other have been entertained, but, meanwhile somebody put her up to a device which opened up quite a new vista of complications, namely, an action in the newly-constituted Supreme Court.†

We thus have an instructive opportunity of comparing Muhammadan law, as we found it in operation in India, with English law in the shape in which it was first trans-

* The proper place of trial was, of course, Patna, but the Faujdari Court there consisted of the Kazi, one of the Muftís, and the Collector, who were all more or less concerned with instituting the prosecution.

† Behader Beg was held amenable to the jurisdiction owing to the accident of his having become surety for the collection of revenues, though the dispute had nothing whatever to do with the Government revenue ; and the Kazi and Muftis by reason of their holding office under the Company, though the very ground of their condemnation was that they were held to be mere private individuals in respect of the particular acts complained of.

planted into India; though it cannot be said that either system presents itself entirely unmixed with the other, and certainly, neither is seen by any means at its best.

The passage quoted from Bentham, at the head of the preceding chapter, was there applied to Muhammadan law in India, but its original application was to English law in India, and the essay in which it occurs (written in 1782) appears to have been suggested in part by these very proceedings.

Treatment of the Case by the King's Judges.

"Bad everywhere, and worse for being transplanted," must certainly be our verdict on the rule* which authorised the arrest of the defendants at the very beginning of the proceedings, from which they were only released through being bailed by the Company. Still worse was the rule of evidence * which debarred both plaintiff and defendants from being examined as witnesses. This alone would be enough to destroy all confidence in the conclusions arrived at by the Court; but if the English law had been applied in its entirety things would have been in one sense worse, in another sense better, because Kojah Zekeriah, the principal witness on the plaintiff's side, would also have been excluded, as taking an interest * under one of the deeds set up by her, so that a nonsuit would have been inevitable. The objection was not, however, taken by counsel, and, in accordance with another English practice which is only tolerable where good lawyers are plentiful, it was no business of the Court to elicit by its own exertions evidence not tendered by the parties. Thus the burden of proof became the most vital of all questions, and a mistake on that point rendered a correct adjudication on the merits impossible.

One important part of English civil procedure was *not*

* These rules were abolished in England in 1838, 1851, and 1843 respectively.

transplanted, namely, trial by jury. Criminal trials before the Supreme Court were by jury, the jury being exclusively British, an arrangement as entirely contrary to the spirit of the institution as if it had been enacted in England that the jurors should always be Frenchmen. An extension of this system to civil cases was at one time demanded by the Europeans at Calcutta, but very properly refused,* and native jurors were out of the question, unless judges could be found capable of summing-up to them in their own language. None the less does this unavoidable mutilation of the system supply an additional reason for pronouncing it "the worse for being transplanted." The judgment of the Court contains absurdities which would have been at once apparent to a jury acquainted with the habits and institutions of the country.

As regards the substantive law applied to the case, "we likewise," said Sir Elijah Impey, "are of opinion that cases of property, when the question depends upon the Muhammadan law, should be determined by the rules of that law; for which purpose we have Moluvies attending upon us to whom we refer such questions, and their opinions become guides to our judgments." But, though he said this, he did not act upon it. His long, rambling judgment gives no hint of any reference to the Court Moluvies, yet it contains several incidental betrayals of ignorance, and the conclusion finally arrived at was absolutely irreconcilable with the Muhammadan law. For it was in effect that the widow was from the moment of her husband's death, if not before, in lawful possession of the whole of his property, so that any interference with it on the part of any of the defendants was a trespass; and this on the strength of two instruments which may or may not have been forged, but were certainly mere nullities according to the Shariat. Apart from these deeds she was only a fractional heir, and anyone acting on behalf of the absent co-heir, *a fortiori* his son, had a clear right to

---

* Stephen, Nuncomar and Impey, ii. 59, 205.

prevent her from appropriating any of the goods before they had been properly inventoried and divided.

The English law of the period shows to no better advantage when we come to the execution of the decree. Muhammadan law,* like *modern* English law, authorises imprisonment of a judgment debtor only when he has the means of paying and won't pay. In this case all the defendants were at once brought down from Patna to Calcutta, and all except the Kazi, who died on the way, were imprisoned in the common jail without any inquiry as to their ability, and remained there till the whole of the enormous damages awarded against them were paid by the Company.† As the curtain falls on this confused drama, we obtain a glimpse of Allum Beg coming all the way from Cabul to look after his own and his son's interests, and vehemently complaining that both his personal effects and the share of his brother's estate had been forcibly seized by people from Calcutta, professing to act on behalf of the widow. His rights could not, on English principles, be affected by the judgment of a foreign Court in a mere action for damages to which he was not a party; but whether he obtained any redress, or whether the property so seized was allowed for in the settlement by the Company, does not appear.

If the forgery trial, which had been suspended in order to enable Kojah Zekeriah to give evidence at Calcutta, had now been resumed in due course before the Nizámat Adálat at Murshídabád, we should have had some further remarkable contrasts. But the members of the Provincial Council, stung by a taunt of Impey's as to the subserviency of

---

* "Hedaya," Grady's Edition, p. 338.

† They seem to have remained in prison for some years, which I can only account for by supposing that the Company would not pay so long as they had any hope of the decree being reversed. The Company also paid the damages awarded in a separate action by the widow against the members of the Provincial Council.

the "Black Courts," and forgetting the fable of the dog and his shadow, abandoned the Murshídabád prosecution, and indicted the same parties, together with the widow, before the Supreme Court: not, as Impey had challenged them to do, for perjury, committed before him at Calcutta, but for the original forgery at Patna. Such an indictment was naturally quashed, as it could not allege that the forgery was committed at Calcutta, nor by inhabitants of Calcutta, nor by servants of the Company.

The last card left for the defeated side to play, as far as law-courts were concerned, was an appeal to the King in Council, and an appeal was, in fact, entered on their behalf by the East India Company, but it was never pressed to a hearing, and was, at last, in 1789, dismissed for want of prosecution. There was a personal cause sufficient to account for this in the reconciliation of Hastings with Impey; but, apart from that, the unreformed Privy Council of that period was even more incompetent to deal with a cause of this kind than the Supreme Court itself. Indeed, it hardly deserved the name of a judicial body. The very meeting at which this appeal was dismissed was held at Windsor, and attended by the King in person, by the Prime Minister, and by a number of noble lords, hardly any of whom appear to have held high judicial office.;* and though the legal element would, no doubt, have been rather more prominent at the actual hearing, there was little to encourage the hope that the gravity of the mistake made by the Supreme Court in neglecting to inform itself as to the Muhammadan Law bearing upon the case would be properly appreciated. The general want of confidence is shown by the fact that not a single appeal from India was heard between 1773 and 1799, and from 1799 to 1833 only fifty from the Supreme Court, and none from the Company's Courts.†

---

* Memoirs of Sir E. Impey, by his son, p. 346.

† Morley's "Digest." Introd., p. 24.

The Act of 1781. *Different systems for Calcutta, and for the Provinces, but native laws recognised in both.*

The practical question was, how to prevent for the future such costly miscarriages of justice as occurred in the Patna case; and it was at last recognised that the law to be administered to the natives of Bengal must be accommodated to their habits and expectations, and must not be simply English law transplanted whole. But through what agency was this to be done? it was obvious that the British Parliament had neither the knowledge nor the leisure to frame suitable laws for Bengal; and the choice lay between throwing upon English lawyers, sent out as the King's Judges, the task of adapting English law to the new conditions, or on the other hand taking the Native laws as the standing point, and requiring the Company's servants to master them and supervise their application, and the Company's Government to introduce such modifications as justice or expediency might require. Now, although the Company's servants had hitherto done very badly when told off to exercise, in the intervals of other business, judicial functions for which they had had no sort of training, still, their length of stay in the country afforded a hope that it might be possible to make it worth the while of some of them to acquire the necessary qualifications. On the other hand, in order to attract a sufficient number of really competent and adaptable English lawyers, salaries out of all proportion to the resources of the country, representing the compensation for throwing themselves completely out of the race for home preferment, would be indispensable; and, in either case, unfortunately, the European colony was sure to object to being rendered amenable to the same laws and law-courts as the natives. Accordingly, by the Act of 1781 (21 George III., c. 70), the jurisdiction of the Supreme Court was confined, so far as natives were concerned, to the town of Calcutta, and it was provided that, even there, "their succession and inheritance to lands, rents, and goods, and all matters of contract and dealing between party and party, should be determined, in the case of Mahomedans, by the laws and usages of the Mahomedans; and, in the case of Gentoos (Hindús), by the laws and usages of the Gentoos." Another clause qualified the application of the English criminal law to native inhabitants of Calcutta, by declaring that "the rights of fathers and masters of families, as the same might have been exercised by the laws of Gentoos or the Mahomedan law,"* should be preserved. Power was also expressly given to the Supreme Court to accommodate the rules of procedure to the religion and manners of the natives.

On the other hand, the Act expressly recognised and defined the power of the Governor-General in Council to constitute Provincial Courts of Justice, to appoint a committee of Council to hear appeals therefrom, and to frame regulations for the guidance of those Courts, subject only to disallowance by the Privy Council; and Warren Hastings naturally made use of these powers to confirm the footing on which the Muhammadan Law had been placed by his regulations of 1772. That is, the Muhammadan Criminal Law was taken to be the general law of the land, as well for Hindús as for Muhammadans, and, in fact, continued for some years more to be worked by native officers under the control of the Nawáb, while the Muhammadan Civil Law supplied the rule of decision for the bulk of the litigation between Muhammadans, but had no application whatever to non-Muhammadans.

Gradual Modification and Ultimate Abolition of Muhammadan Criminal Law in Bengal.

The following extract from Busteed's "Echoes of Old Calcutta" (p. 138) may serve to give an idea of the Muhammadan criminal tribunals as they existed in 1789, while still in purely native hands, English influence only

* Thus recognising, among other things, the Muhammadan institution of slavery, which the British Government did not abolish till 1843.

operating intermittently through the Resident at Murshídabád, and English officers acting normally as their thief-catchers.

" *The Calcutta Chronicle* in the following year (1789) gives a terrible account of the example which was made of a gang of dacoits. Fourteen were sent by a Mr. Redfern from Kishnagur to Salkey to take their trial at the (native) Faujdari Court. On being found guilty, the following sentence was ordered to be carried out at Sair Bazaar, near Calcutta, on the Howrah side of the river: each man to have his right hand and left foot cut off at the joint.* The victims were taken one by one, each in sight of the others, and pinioned to the ground; a fillet or band was then laid over the mouth to drown the cries. The amputation was most clumsily performed with an instrument like a carving-knife to find out the joint; each limb took about three minutes. The stumps were then dipped in hot ghee, and the criminal left to his fate. None died under the operation; four died soon after, but more (it is said) from the effects of the sun and neglect than from the savage severity which was applied. *The Chronicle* regrets the necessity for such

---

* This sentence was in strict accordance with the law as laid down by both Hanáfi and Máliki authorities. See "Harrington's Analysis", i., 316; D'Ohsson, "Tableau de l'Empire Ottoman," iii. 260; Seignette, "Code Musulman," par Khalil, s. 2,014. It is partially supported by the Koran, chap. v., Sale, pp. 77, 78. According to Mr. Milner ("England in Egypt," p. 381), as late as 1890, in the semi-elective Legislative Council of Egypt, an amendment to a Government Bill for the more effectual punishment of brigandage received the support of all the non-official members, which was to the effect that, in accordance with the religious law, any brigand arrested before he had committed theft or homicide should, after being submitted to the bastinado, be imprisoned until he repented or died; that any brigand who had committed theft without murder should have his right hand and left foot cut off; and, lastly, that any brigand who had committed murder should be punishable at the choice of the authorities either (1) by amputation of the right hand and left foot, followed by execution, or (2) by amputation, followed by crucifixion; or (3) by amputation, followed by execution and crucifixion (*sic*); or (4) by simple execution; or (5) by simple crucifixion.

examples, but blesses God that they are not authorised by the laws of England.*

I have been told, but have not verified the statement, that among the old records at Chittagong is a letter from Warren Hastings to the Collector, who had consulted him about a threatened execution by impalement, to the effect that, though his sentiments of humanity do him honour, he must not attempt to interfere with the course of native justice.†

In 1790 the criminal jurisdiction was withdrawn from the Nawáb Nazím, and brought under the direct control of the Company, which had itself been by this time brought more directly under the control of the British Government. Courts of Circuit were established, but were changed in 1793 into stationary District Courts, consisting of a civil servant of the Company bearing the title of Judge, a Kazi, and a Muftí. The evidence was to be heard in presence of all three. The fatwa, or declaration of the law applicable to the case, was to be written at the bottom of the record by the Kazi and Muftí. It was the duty of the judge to carefully consider the fatwa, and, if it appeared to him consonant to natural justice and to the Muhammadan Law, to pass sentence accordingly, and issue his warrant to the magistrate for execution, except when the sentence was of death or perpetual imprisonment, in which case it would require confirmation by the Sadr Nizámat Adálat—afterwards amalga-

* The English criminal law of this period was, however, taken as a whole, considerably more severe than the Muhammadan. It was not till the following year (1790) that the punishments of disembowelling, &c., for high treason, and of burning women alive for petty treason were abolished. Simple capital punishment continued to be much more largely employed for another half century; while imprisonment and transportation were for the most part so managed as to be more cruel but less exemplary than mutilation, and much more costly.

† Impalement is understood by some Moslems to be one of the punishments authorised by the Koranic expression, "they shall be crucified," and was formerly not very uncommon in Turkey. It was a Persian practice long before Islam. It was prohibited by Akbar, as was also mutilation.

mated with the Sadr Diwáni Adálat, and called simply the Sadr Adálat. In case of the fatwa appearing to the judge to be contrary either to natural justice or to the Muhammadan Law, he was to transmit the proceedings to the Court of Appeal, stating his objections thereto. If the latter Court considered the sentence to be in accordance with Muhammadan Law but contrary to natural justice, they were to adhere thereto if in favour of the prisoner, but if against him, to recommend a pardon or mitigation of sentence, and at the same time to propose a new regulation to provide against a recurrence of the case. Down to 1801 this Sadr Court consisted of the Governor-General and Council with a Chief Kazi and two Muftís, but it was then strengthened by the addition of judges who were to be covenanted civilians but not members of Council. The function of the Sadr Nizámat Adálat as originally constituted, presumably, therefore, of the Sadr Court on its criminal side, was "to exercise the powers of the Nawáb Nazím, leaving the declaration of the law, as applicable to the circumstances of the case, to the chief Kazi and Muftís, agreeably to former practice." Ultimately only one native law-officer was attached to each District Court. Successive regulations of the Bengal Government pruned off one by one the most archaic peculiarities of the Muhammadan criminal law. Thus, in 1791, imprisonment with hard labour was substituted for mutilation.* In 1792 prosecutions for murder ceased to depend on the concurrence of the murdered man's relatives. In 1801 the curious rule was abrogated that a person who intended to kill A but accidentally killed B instead, was not punishable capitally either for what he intended or for what he actually did. In 1822 it was enacted that "the justificatory plea that the person

* Seven years being the equivalent for loss of one limb, fourteen for two. Whether this was an improvement or otherwise, would depend on the way the prisons were managed, as to which I have no information. See the note on the preceding page.

murdered was the mistress or relation of the prisoner, and detected in criminal intercourse with another man, or that the murdered man was found in criminal intercourse with the prisoner's mistress or relation, or generally speaking, detected in fornication, shall not be upheld in bar of capital punishment"; thus overruling a fatwa which had been followed by the Sadr Court in 1820, to the effect that the killing of a sister and her paramour in the act of fornication was justifiable homicide. Again, so late as 1833, a fatwa to the effect that a prisoner could not be convicted on the evidence of a female and a minor was apparently acted on; but a similar fatwa, given in 1835 was overruled by the Sadr Court, without, so far as appears, any intervening legislation.*

It does not appear that the practice of actually handing over the murderer for execution to the relatives of the murdered person, as "avengers of blood," was ever resorted to under British rule, though it is undoubted Muhammadan Law.† Lastly, the rule of evidence excluding the testimony of Moslems against non-Moslems was of course not allowed to prevail, but it was so far respected that such cases were to be reported to the Appellate Court, with a statement by the law-officers as to what their fatwa would have been if the witnesses had been Muhammadans.

In 1832 it was enacted that non-Muhammadans should not be tried according to Muhammadan Law for offences cognisable under the general Regulations. What offences were so cognisable it is not easy to make out, nor is it now very material to know; inasmuch as every trace of the old system disappeared with the enactment, in 1860, of a general Penal Code for British India, to which not only

* All these examples are taken from Morley's "Digest," Vol. I., heading "Criminal Law."

† Seignette, "Code Musulman, par Khalil," s. 1703.

Hindús but Europeans are amenable equally with Muhammadans. The Code was recorded complete in 1838, and the remarks then made by its framers on the system they were proposing to supersede are worth quoting.

"The penal law of Bengal and of the Madras Presidency is in fact Mahomedan Law, which has gradually been distorted to such an extent as to deprive it of all title to the religious veneration of Mahomedans, yet which retains enough of its original peculiarities to perplex and encumber the administration of justice. In substance it now differs at least as widely from the Mahomedan Penal Law, as the penal law of England differs from the penal law of France. Yet technical terms and nice distinctions borrowed from the Muhammadan Law are still retained. Nothing is more usual than for the Courts to ask the law-officers what punishment the Mahomedan law prescribes in a hypothetical case, and then to inflict that punishment on a person who is not within that hypothetical case, and who by the Mahomedan Law would be liable either to a different punishment or to no punishment. We by no means presume to condemn the policy which led the British Government to retain, and gradually to modify, the system of criminal jurisprudence which it found established in these provinces. But it is evident that a body of law thus formed must, considered merely as a body of law, be defective and inconvenient."

I am inclined to think that the Penal Code itself, excellent as it is, and successfully as it has been worked on the whole, would have been yet more successful if Muhammadan lawyers had been heard in argument against some of its provisions before they were passed. For instance, the anomalous nature of the clause* which provides punishment for the male paramour (married or unmarried) of a married

---

*I.P.C., s. 497. The Draft Penal Code of Hyderabad, referred to below, deals with adultery under the head of offences against the rights of guardians, the husband being considered as the guardian of the wife, and punishes both her and the paramour, but the latter more severely.

woman, while the woman goes off scot-free, would have been set in a more striking light by being contrasted with the stern consistency of the Korán, which prescribes capital punishment for adultery on the part of married persons of either sex, and the minor punishment of scourging for the unmarried accomplice of either sex.

The Hyderabad Penal Code.

In the Nizám's dominions, that large fragment of the Mogul empire which is still governed by a Muhammadan dynasty under British protection, the Muhammadan Criminal Law naturally still keeps its place as the acknowledged substratum of the system actually administered; but there also it has been gradually overlaid by regulations influenced in no small degree by modern European notions. The Indian Penal Code itself was a few years ago translated into Urdu in order to enable the Government to determine how far it would be suitable for adoption, but the conclusion arrived at that "even the best law imported wholesale from outside can never be permanent nor very useful"; and instead thereof a code was drafted in 1891, avowedly on the basis of the local law already in force, but "with such modifications as appear to be required or commended by the just dictates and wise teachings of the Mahomedan Law and Mahomedan jurists, or by the advanced and more humane notions of European jurists that have within the last century revolutionised the criminal law of the civilised world." I have not seen the draft itself, but by the courtesy of the Home Secretary to the Nizám's Government I have been furnished with the "statement of objects and reasons," which may be assumed to give a fair idea of its nature, and certainly shows a remarkable degree of emancipation from the letter of the Shariat, on the part of a body of professedly Moslem statesmen. That free hand in legislation which Akbar could only secure by throwing over Islam altogether, seems to be in this case enjoyed as a result of the State's dependence on the protection of a non-Muhammadan paramount power. Such at least will be the inference, if and when the projected Code has actually become law.

Muhammadan Civil Law, how far preserved.

As regards the substantive civil law, the original regulation of Warren Hastings, specifying disputes respecting "inheritance, marriage, and caste, and any [other] religious usage or institution," as those which were to be determined according to the personal laws of Hindús and Muhammadans respectively, has remained substantially unchanged down to the present day, re-appearing with only the omission of the word "other" in the "Bengal N. W. P., and Assam Civil Courts Act" of 1871, and again in the corresponding Act of 1887. The more extensive list of topics set forth in the Charter of 1781 for the guidance of the Supreme Court in suits against native inhabitants of Calcutta survived the disappearance, in 1861, of the Supreme Court as a distinct tribunal, the old original civil jurisdiction being transferred unchanged to the new High Court; but in practice there has never been much difference between the town of Calcutta and the Mufassal.* The Company's judges might plausibly have argued that any rule found in the Shariat, whether about contract or any other subject, must be within their cognisance as matter of religious institution, unless expressly provided for by Regulations, and this line has in fact been taken in recent times by one judge of the High Court; but they preferred the conveniently vague principle that "justice, equity, and good conscience" should be their guide in all doubtful cases, and that it was equitable to interpret contracts between Muhammadans with reference to the law which the contracting parties presumably had in their minds.

---

* Mufassal, corruptly Mofussil, separate, distinct, particular: in Hindustán, a subordinate or separate district; its most usual application in Bengal is to the country in general as distinct from Calcutta. Wilson.

When, in 1872, the Indian Legislature passed a general Contract Act, modelled in most respects on the English law, this manifestly superseded all reference to Muhammadan contract law in the Mufassal, and was interpreted (very conveniently but not without considerable straining of its language) to have the same effect in Calcutta.

Hence, whereas Macnaghten's "Principles and Precedents of Moohummudan Law," published in 1825, includes a collection of Precedents on "Sale," on "Debts and Securities," and on "Claims and Judicial Matters," and Mr. Baillie thought it worth while to publish in 1850 a text-book on the Muhammadan Law of Sale, Woodman's Digest, published under the orders of Government in 1887-8, gives no corresponding subdivision of the title "Muhammadan Law." It is, however, still, for some mysterious reason, included in the law course of the Calcutta University.*

The range of Anglo-Muhammadan Law was defined somewhat differently, and with more detail, in the enactments governing the Panjab, Oudh, and the Central Provinces respectively, but its actual working appears to be much the same, with two exceptions. The first is that in the Panjab the Muhammadans and Hindús have become so intermixed that tribes professing different religions are often found conforming to the same civil usages, and as the Courts are directed to look to local custom in the first instance and only to fall back upon the Korán or the Shasters where customary law is silent, the occasions for applying the pure Muhammadan Law are comparatively rare. The second is that in Oudh the particular form of Muhammadan Law most generally administered is that of the Isna-Asharya Shias.†

Shia Law in Oudh.

The historical explanation of the last-mentioned peculiarity is as follows. The Muhammadan kingdoms of the

* See "Ameer Ali's Student's Handbook," p. 107, note.

† As to these, see chap. iii.

Deccan had been the chief Shia strongholds down to their conquest by Aurangzíb; but, in the confusion that followed, so much of them as could be rescued from the Maráthas fell to the lot of the so-called Nizám ul Mulk, a Sunní, whose descendants still rule there under British protection. On the other hand, the chief political rival of the Nizám was one Saadat Ali Khan, originally a Persian merchant of Khorassan, and consequently a Shia by religion. His heterodoxy did not prevent his holding under a Sunní Emperor both the office of Vizier, or Prime Minister, of the Empire and the Viceroyalty or Subahdarship of the great province of Oudh, then comprising nearly everything between Delhi and the frontier of Bahar, and transmitting both dignities to his descendants, who were also Shias. So long as those "Nawáb Viziers" were content with that title, and held nominally under the Mogul Emperor, though really, from 1765 downwards, under the British Government, the Sunní law, as the general law of the Empire, continued to be administered in their dominions, nor was any formal change made for many years after their assumption in 1818 of the title of King. But the number of professed Shias naturally continued to increase under Court influence, and at last, in 1847, nine years before the British annexation, a Shia Muftí was appointed, and that law was applied in all cases where either party was a Shia.*

Under British rule the practice in Oudh and everywhere else is to administer the law of the school or sect to which the person who is the common root of title belonged, but whereas elsewhere the burden of proof is on those who assert themselves to be Shias, in Oudh it is the other way.

Bombay and Madras.

The enactments above mentioned applied exclusively to the Bengal Presidency, or parts thereof. The vicissitudes

* "Tagore Lectures," of 1874, by Shamachurn Sircar, p. 175, note. Elphinstone's "India," Book XII., chap. ii., 3, 4.

which Muhammadan Law underwent in the two minor Presidencies followed a parallel course in the main, but present some special features.

Both had the double system of judicature, consisting of a Supreme Court for the Presidency Town, and a graded system of Company's Courts for the Mufassal; but the Supreme Courts of Madras and Bombay were not constituted till long after the conflict of jurisdictions had been fought out in Bengal—Madras, 1800; Bombay, 1823—so that their charters naturally followed the modest pattern of 1781, in preference to that of 1773. In the case of Bombay, the correspondence was exact; the Madras Charter differed chiefly by declaring that the questions of inheritance, contract, etc., should be determined *either* by the laws and usages of Muhammadans or Gentoos, as the case might be, *or*, "by such laws and usages as the same would have been determined by if the suit had been brought in a native court," meaning, apparently, one of the Company's Mufassal Courts, thus guarding against any serious divergence between the practice of the two sets of tribunals in native cases.

As regards the Madras Mufassal, the original Regulations of 1802 were copied from the Bengal Regulations of 1790, and included the rule laid down by Hastings in 1772 as to the matters to be determined according to the law of the Korán, or of the Shasters, in civil suits. A clause to the same effect was inserted in the Madras Civil Courts' Act of 1873, and thence transferred, with the addition of words referring to Buddhist Law, to the Burma Courts Act of 1875. The same Regulations adopted the Bengal modifications of the Muhammadan Criminal Law so far as they had gone at that date, and the subsequent history of the system was very similar.

The Bombay Presidency had no Mufassal worth speaking of until after the third Marátha war (1818); and as the territories then acquired had been for a century or so under Hindú rule we did not find the Muhammadan criminal law generally in force as such, however much of the prevailing practice may have been really of Muhammadan origin. Elphinstone's Criminal Code, which came into force in 1827, and was only superseded by the general Penal Code in 1860, may be described roughly as the existing native usage passed through a Benthamite sieve, and one remarkable section admits within certain limits the characteristically Hindú notion of separate criminal laws for separate religions.

"Offences declared penal by the religious law of the person charged, provided they be not included among those for which punishment is enacted in the code of regulations, but, nevertheless, constitute a breach of morality, or of the peace or good order of society, shall be liable to such punishment as may be prescribed by the religious law of the convict, if it be of a nature authorised by s. 3 of this regulation. Otherwise, it shall be commuted to such of the punishments therein authorised as may be deemed equivalent and appropriate by the authority taking cognisance of the case.*

As regards the recognition of native laws, in the Civil Courts, Elphinstone's Bombay Regulations deviated from the Bengal model precisely in the same point which was, afterwards insisted on by the Panjab administrators, namely by giving precedence to local usage over the written Muhammadan or Hindú Law. "The law to be observed in the trial of suits shall be Acts of Parliament and Regulations of Government applicable to the case; in the absence of such Acts and Regulations, the usage of the country in which the suit arose; if none such appears, the law of the defendant, and, in the absence of specific law and usage, justice, equity, and good conscience alone," Reg. iv. of 1826, s. 26 (still in force). Probably, what the legislator had chiefly in view was, to protect the multifarious usages of low-caste Hindús

* Reg. xiv. of 1827, s. 1 (7). It is not easy to put a case which would satisfy all the conditions. Would wine-drinking by a Muhammadan, or cow-killing by a Hindú, be considered "breaches of morality, or of the peace or good order of society?"

from being forced into Procrustean conformity with the strict Brahminical standard; but since that time, actual litigation has brought to light the existence of two considerable bodies of professed Muhammadans, whose ancestors were converts from Hindúism, but who never exchanged the Hindú law of inheritance for that of the Korán; while another large class of trading Muhammadans, called Borahs, are said to be Ismalian Shías, on whose usages none of the ordinary law-books would throw much light.

Measures for the ascertainment of Muhammadan Law.

So able a man as Hastings was not likely to miss the lesson of the Patna case as to the danger and discredit of entire ignorance of the native laws on the part of Europeans exercising judicial functions; and as these laws were locked up in two difficult languages only known to the learned among the natives themselves, he saw that the best plan was to have the most authoritative text-books translated into English. He naturally thought first of the Fatáwa Alamgírí,* as the most important compilation made by and for the Moslems of India; but further examination showed it to be less adapted for the instruction of Englishmen than the Hedaya. As the Arabic of the latter was considered to be too difficult for an English scholar to render directly into his own language, three Muhammadan Maulawis were employed to translate the work into Persian, and then this translation, with the notes of the translators, was done into English by Mr. Hamilton, a servant of the Company. His work was completed in 1791, and gratefully dedicated to Hastings, who had returned to England some years before and was then undergoing impeachment.

It so happened however that the Hedaya, or at least the Indian copies thereof, contained no chapters on the subject of Inheritance, the most important of all for the Anglo-Indian Civil Courts. Either no such chapters had ever been

---

* See Chap. iv. p. 85.

written, though the plan of the work seems intended to be exhaustive, or they had been superseded by special treatises and therefore ceased to be reproduced. Two such monographs were found to be in use, called the Sirajjiyah and the Sharifyah, both emanating, like the Hedaya, from the law schools at Transoxiana, and the latter of the two said to date from 1410 A.D., or thereabouts. Both were translated from Arabic into Persian by a learned Muhammadan under the auspices of Warren Hastings, and not long afterwards (1792) Sir William Jones, with the sanction of Lord Cornwallis, made an English translation of the Sirajjiyah direct from the Arabic, and an abstract of the Sharifyah.*

It will readily be understood that these literary undertakings did not for a long time produce any very marked effect on the administration of justice. Before criticism of the native law-officers could become really effective, it was necessary to watch their course of practice during a considerable period, to record their decisions, and gradually, by comparing them with each other, and with the authorities on which they were supposed to rest, and sifting out those which would not stand the test, to build up a body of law ascertained to be in conformity with the actual expectations of the Muhammadans of India. The most effective contribution to this object was the work published in 1825, by Mr. W. H. Macnaghten, entitled "Principles and Precedents of Muhammadan Law." The "Precedents" are selected legal opinions given in reply to questions put by the Company's judges in the Bengal Presidency, and therefore of course turning upon points raised in actual litigation. The "Principles" are the author's generalisations from these opinions. The bulk of the work is concerned with Hanáfi law, but there is a brief summary of the Shia law

---

*Though the Fatáwa Alámgírí has never been formally translated, the effect of considerable portions is given in Baillie's "Digest" and in his "Moohummudan Law of Sale."

with corresponding Precedents, showing that even in Bengal at that date the Shias were strong enough to attract attention. It remained for many years the standard work on all the branches of Muhammadan Civil Law then recognised by the Courts.

Anglo-Muhammadan Judiciary Law.

But the kind of case-law embodied in Macnaghten's Precedents began itself to be gradually superseded by case-law of the English type—professorial case-law by judge-made case-law. Though the decisions of the British Courts were based upon fatwas, they owed their force as precedents, according to English notions, rather to the judges who actually pronounced them than to the Muftís who were consulted about them, and some of these decisions had begun to be reported by private enterprise even before the publication of the "Principles and Precedents." A collection of notes of cases decided in the Supreme Court goes back to 1813, and Mr. Macnaghten himself published in 1827 two volumes of reports of cases decided in the Company's Courts. Once in print, of course these reports soon began to be referred to as authorities; and though, considering the necessarily imperfect knowledge of the judges who were thus immortalised, their successors felt much less scruple about overruling them than they would have been expected to show in England, still, when once a beginning had been made, the chain of judicial authority grew continually stronger and tighter. The process was very materially aided by the action of the Judicial Committee of the Privy Council, as constituted by the Act 3 and 4 William IV. c. 41 (1833). Freed from the intrusion of lay politicians, and re-inforced by ex-judges of the Indian Supreme Courts as assessors, it soon began to command high respect for its decisions in the comparatively small number of cases which the parties could afford to bring before it. And though the

Muhammadan cases with which it had to deal were very few as compared with those arising between Hindús, the mere possibility of appeal tended to make the Indian Courts more careful and consistent. The constitution of the four High Courts in 1861 worked strongly in the same direction by bringing together on the same bench the barrister-judges sent out from England and the leaders of the judicial branch of the Indian Civil Service, hitherto kept entirely apart in the Supreme and Sadr Courts respectively, and by joining with both the *élite* of Indian practitioners.

Abolition of the Court Maulawis.

At last, in 1864, the Government felt itself strong enough to dispense with the services of the Muhammadan law-officers altogether, and since then all questions depending upon that law have been determined, like other questions, by the Court itself, after hearing the arguments of counsel, who may or may not happen to be Muhammadans. At the present time Muhammadans are to be found not only at the bar and in subordinate judicial positions, but on the benches of High Courts; and the rulings of tribunals so composed and so assisted, embodied since 1876 in authorised reports, perhaps give as much satisfaction to the Muhammadan community as could have been given by the fatwas of the most learned of Muftís under the limitations imposed by the essentially hybrid character of Anglo-Muhammadan Law.

Legislative Innovations.

How impossible it is for a detached portion of a legal system, however scrupulously protected from formal change, to go on working out the same social results as before, when other parts of the system have been fundamentally altered, will be shown by one or two examples in the next chapter, and will appear more fully in the Digest. But, besides this indirect operation of new surroundings and new methods of applying the law to the facts, the direct and avowed legislative innovations within the range of the reserved topics have been very important though not very numerous. It must suffice here merely to name by way of example the Freedom of Religion Act, 1850, and the Guardians and Wards Act, 1890.

The Need of Codification.

Certainly the present state of things bears no stamp of finality about it. Though we have already abolished all parts of the law of Islam which trench in any way on the rights of non-Muhammadans, and most of what seriously offends against British notions of natural justice, and though the family and inheritance law which we continue to enforce would not, perhaps, strike an impartial foreigner as much worse than the corresponding portion of English law, still there are not wanting indications of a reform party among the Muhammadans themselves, who may in time be in a position to speak for their co-religionists generally.* But it is earnestly to be hoped that attention to the *form* of Anglo-Muhammadan Law may take precedence of any further tinkering of its *substance.* At present a Muhammadan of British India who wishes to acquaint himself with the laws specially affecting him as such must first consult some English text-book possessing no intrinsic authority whatever; must then, if the statements contained therein are disputed, work back, sometimes to reports of British judicial decisions, credited with various and ill-defined degrees of authority—sometimes

* Mr. Justice Ameer Ali, who claims spiritual affinity with the Motazalas of the Abbasside period (see chap. iii.), stoutly maintains that the true "Spirit of Islam" is antagonistic to polygamy as well as to slavery, and that enthusiastic admiration for Mahomet is quite consistent with rejection of particular precepts as of merely local and temporary application. Whatever we may think of his historical accuracy, or of the soundness of his logic, the appearance of such a book from such a quarter marks a new epoch in the history of Islam.

to fatwas given by nameless Maulawis in the early days of British rule, sometimes to English translations of medieval Arabic treatises, occasionally, perhaps, to Arabic treatises still untranslated, and must pay, or make his opponent pay, for all the skilled labour employed in the inquiry. Such a system is indeed difficult to defend, except by the *tu quoque* method of pointing out that the condition of Anglo-Hindú Law is considerably worse and that of some branches of English Law not much better.* It was otherwise when we said in effect to the two great native communities, "We don't profess to understand your scriptures, nor your methods of interpretation, but we will trust your accredited representatives to tell us what the decision should be in each case as it arises." But we have long ago abandoned that attitude, and cannot now disclaim responsibility for what has come to be in great part our own handiwork.† More than half a century ago, when this was much less obvious, the straightforward course of codifying the laws intended to be administered to Hindús and Muhammadans respectively was resolved on, but, unfortunately, not persevered with. Macaulay, in his famous minute on Indian education (1835), having occasion to notice the argument based by the Orientalists on "the fact that the Hindú Law is chiefly to be learnt from Sanskrit books, and the Muhammadan Law from Arabic books," remarked as follows:—

"We are commanded by Parliament to ascertain and digest the laws of India. The assistance of a Law Com-

---

* Perhaps the rules of inheritance should be excepted from the above remarks. In this branch, owing to the completeness and precision of the Muhammadan authorities and of the English text-books founded thereon, and also owing to its being untouched (except in one point) by British legislation, little practical inconvenience results from the want of a code.

† The question whether British India, as a country ruled by an infidel Government which permit the free exercise of Moslem worship and preaching, and which enforces through its tribunals a part of the Muhammadan

mission has been given to us for that purpose. As soon as the code is promulgated the Shasters and the Hedaya will be useless to a Munsif or Sadr Amín. I hope and trust that before the boys who are now entering at the Madrasa and the Sanskrit College have completed their studies this great work will be finished. It would be manifestly absurd to educate the rising generation with a view to a state of things which we mean to alter before they reach manhood."*

As is well known, even the Penal Code framed by this Law Commission hung fire till 1860, and when at last the work of codification was resumed with some degree of energy, the codifiers still showed, as they do to this day, a disposition to postpone indefinitely the application of the process to the two great bodies of personal law which still rest avowedly on a Scriptural basis. The manifestations of this feeling have, so far as I know, come entirely from the British side. In 1882 Sir Syed Ahmed Khan bore emphatic testimony in the Legislative Council of India to the general desire of the natives to have their laws codified, and so far as the sentiments of educated Muhammadans are concerned we could hardly have a more competent witness.† The British scruples appear not to spring from any special tenderness for native institutions as they are, but, on the contrary, from an unwillingness to assume that more direct and conspicuous responsibility for them which would be implied from our re-stating their rules in language of our

civil law, ought to be regarded as Dar ul Islam or as Darul Harb (the country of hostility), was very earnestly discussed about twenty years ago. See Hunter's "Indian Musalmans," and the reply to the same by Syed Ahmed Khan (now Sir Syed Ahmed). The latter seems to establish that the above classification is not an exhaustive one, and that a country does not necessarily become Dar ul Harb, so as to render it the duty of the faithful to abandon it or to make war upon it, merely because it has ceased to be, in the full sense, Dar ul Islam.

* Quoted in Boulger's "Memoir of Lord William Bentinck," Rulers of India Series. Clarendon Press, Oxford, 1892.

† See the passage quoted in Stokes's "Anglo-Indian Codes," Vol. I., Introd. p. 21.

own selection. One might sympathise with this feeling if there were any solid foundation for what seems to be a common notion among Anglo-Indian administrators, that to codify is to stereotype, but there is not. The natural effect of clear and methodical statement is to facilitate criticism and to stimulate demands for reform, and such has been the result in the case of every large code yet passed for India. The only peculiarity in the case of personal laws exclusively affecting particular sections of the population is that it is a simpler matter for the ruling power to ascertain and give effect to their wishes. The difficulties in the way of a general representative system for India do not apply to subordinate representative assemblies for castes and sects requiring special legislation, and an example on a small scale of the kind of thing required was afforded as far back as 1806 by Sir Alexander Johnston as Governor of Ceylon.* More recently the Parsís have obtained by instalments (1837, 1865, and 1872) what is practically a code of inheritance and marriage law on the lines suggested by themselves. The codification of Anglo-Muhammadan Law would not only be a much more serious undertaking than either of these by reason of its affecting nearly fifty million souls, but it would also be rather different in kind, because it would not deal with unwritten usage to be gathered from the lips of living witnesses, nor primarily with sentiments to be gathered from the votes of living members, but with the mass of hetero-

* "Ceylon Ordinances" (ed. 1874). Extract from the minutes of a Council held at Colombo, August 5th, 1806. "The Chief Justice submits to the Governor in Council the Code of Muhammadan Laws observed by the Moors in the province of Colombo, and acknowledged by the head Moormen of the district to be adapted to the present usages of the caste. *Resolved*, on the motion of the Chief Justice, that the same be published, and that they be observed throughout the whole of the province of Colombo."

My attention was directed to these ordinances and also to the Parsí Acts by a pamphlet entitled "Hindú Law in Bombay: a Plea for its Codification." Bombay, 1872. The author's initials, F. R. V., are those of a Parsí barrister practising at Bombay.

geneous written matter which has accumulated from the first reduction of the Korán to the latest numbers of the Indian Law Reports. On the other hand the problem is considerably less complex and difficult than that of codifying Anglo-Hindú Law, and has so far the best claim to be first taken in hand. The judge-made law to be condensed consists of less than 500 cases, as against upwards of 2,000 cited in the standard text-book of Hindú Law, and the Arabian law-sources are far more compact and homogeneous than the Sanskrit. I shall be very glad if the Digest, to which these chapters are intended to be introductory, should prove in any degree helpful towards the accomplishment of this much-needed reform.

CHAPTER VI.

Brief Outline of Anglo-Muhammadan Law.

"In commencing an exposition of the laws [of the Roman people], the most convenient plan appears to be to give first a slight and simple sketch, and afterwards to explain them in detail, with the greatest possible care and precision."

Institutes of Justinian. Book I., Title i, s. 2.

Marriage.

Those branches of law to which alone this hybrid system is applied in British India, are all more or less closely connected with family relations. The common root of all family relations is, of course, sexual connection, and the law regulating that subject has for its central and most important department, the Law of Marriage. In point of fact, it is not the whole of the Muhammadan Law regulating the relations between the sexes, but only so much of it as bears directly on the institution of marriage, that is recognised and enforced by British Courts.

The legal consequences (when there are any) of extra-matrimonial cohabitation between Muhammadans in British India are not to be ascertained from the Korân or the Hedaya, but from the Penal and Criminal Procedure Codes —with one exception to be presently noticed. The result is, that the balance of the Muhammadan system has been completely upset, and that the practical working of the rules ostensibly derived from that system is very different from anything contemplated by Mahomet or Abu Hanîfa.

The Muhammadan Idea of Marriage.

The spirit of the original system is well indicated by the Arabic word for marriage, and the accepted definition thereof.* According to the Hedaya, "Nikkah," in its primitive sense, means carnal conjunction. As a legal term it was defined in the Kanz—a work of repute, earlier than the Hedaya—as "a contract for the purpose of legalising generation"; which expression, however, a commentator explains as including both the right of enjoyment, and the procreation of children. Of course, all systems of matrimonial law have this for their starting-point. The imperiousness of male desires, and the importance, for the peace of the community, of directing them into safe channels, are considerations which cannot fail to suggest themselves in the very infancy of law; and not much later comes the sense of the value of children as property, and of the expediency of assigning each to some male in particular, together with the woman who is to suckle and rear it. But other systems of law, and still more other systems of religion and ethics, find room as they expand for quite other conceptions of the meaning and purpose of conjugal union. With clearer perception of the difference between good and bad sons, and of the influence of blood and training, comes heightened appreciation of the dignity and responsibilities of motherhood, more care to obtain wives from a good stock, and more disposition to prolong the union at least till the children are grown up. Then, the example of the wiser individuals gives the tone to public opinion and religious beliefs, which ultimately harden into positive law.

Thus an exponent of the ripest jurisprudence of Pagan Rome, two centuries after the first promulgation of Christianity, but a century before its adoption as the State religion, defines marriage as "the union of a male with a female, companionship in respect of the whole of life, participation in divine and human rights and duties"; and three centuries later we find a Law Commission employed by a Christian Emperor to select what might seem most worth preserving from the mass of Pagan legal literature, not only including

* See Baillie, p. 4.

this passage in their larger compilation, but paraphrasing it in a brief elementary text-book.*

The Christian Church in all its branches has always held up this ideal and striven to mould the institutions of the State in conformity therewith. Hindú religion goes further, regarding the matrimonial tie as indissoluble even by death, and as having indeed for its main object felicity in a future life; and Hindú law follows suit, with consequences for good and evil of the weightiest kind.

With Muhammadans, as with Hindús, law is only a particular phase of religion; but neither in their adjustments of civil rights nor in their spiritual counsels of perfection is account taken of any but the two primary objects of the institution of marriage. Re-union of husbands and wives is emphatically *not* among the promised joys of the Moslem paradise, nor do the advantages in this life, to the husband of concentrated domestic affection, and to the children of prolonged maternal care, appear to have impressed themselves at all adequately on the mind of the Prophet. Family life, as modern Englishmen understand the term, was beyond the range of ordinary Arab experience.† According to his lights, and according to the special needs of his time and country, he was a very earnest champion of women's rights; but the ideal for which he strove was merely that of enabling free-born women to pursue under more tolerable conditions the only vocation then open to them, that of child-bearers and child-sucklers; with some slight measure of freedom in choosing their employers, some protection against gross tyranny, some reasonable notice before dismissal, and above all with a substantial pecuniary equivalent for

* Dig. 23, 2, 1, (from Modestinus): Just. I. ix. 1.

† Mahomet's own monogamous connection with Khadija, maintained for some ten years, in fact till her death, may perhaps be cited as an example to the contrary; but the circumstances were altogether exceptional. He was pecuniarily dependent upon her, and instead of taking her to his home was received by her in what is spoken of as her house, but was probably her father's. Muir's "Life of Mahomet," p. 25.

the sacrifices demanded of them. He found them, at least in some tribes, the property of their male kinsmen, to be used, sold, or let to hire like other chattels. He left them, (at least as his precepts were understood by the Hanáfi school) possessed of full legal personality, capable of acquiring property and contracting on their own account, and conversely amenable to the general criminal law, but with their rights of inheritance on the one hand and their punishments on the other restricted in most cases to one-half of those provided for free males.

Leading Features of the System as developed in the Hanafi School.

The gradual working out by the Hanáfi lawyers of the few but important maxims laid down on the above lines in the Korán resulted in a system of which the following are the leading features.

1. All sexual intercourse not expressly permitted by the law is denounced as fornication (*zina*) and incurs very severe penalties, viz., scourging in the case of unmarried and death in the case of married persons of either sex.

2. The connections sanctioned by the law are of two kinds only:—(1) with a wife (or wives, not exceeding four at the same time) regularly married; (2) with female slaves lawfully acquired.

3. Regular marriage is a matter of contract, the terms of which depend, within very wide limits, on the will of the contracting parties, and to the validity of which no religious ceremony is necessary.

Now that the legislature of British India has on the one hand abolished the Muhammadan Criminal Law without substituting any penalties of its own either for simple fornication or for adultery by married persons,* and has on

* The Penal Code, s. 497, provides for the punishment of a male who commits adultery with another man's wife, but not for that of the adulterous wife, nor for that of either of the guilty parties where the adultery is on the part of the husband.

the other hand abolished slavery and with it the possibility of the only kind of concubinage permitted by the Shariat, the stern consistency of the original system has been entirely broken up, and we can only say vaguely that *Anglo-Muhammadan Law* points to a regular contract of marriage as on the whole the most convenient and laudable preliminary to sexual union, and as a generally but perhaps not invariably necessary condition for the establishment of paternity.

The terms of this contract, as implied by law in the absence of special stipulations, are, roughly speaking, that the wife is bound—

to submit to the husband's embraces whenever he requires her to do so, due regard being had to health and decency;

to have no intercourse of any kind with strangers without his permission;

to suckle her children by him if, and only if, he cannot conveniently hire a nurse;

and generally, to conform to his wishes in regard to household arrangements, but not to perform menial services if he can afford to keep servants;

and that the husband is bound—

to give money or money's worth for his marital privileges, part of it immediately and the remainder on the termination of the marriage by death or divorce;

to maintain her suitably to his position during the continuance of the connection; and if he has more than one wife—

to provide each with a separate apartment,

and as far as possible to distribute his attentions equally among them.

Dower.

The above-mentioned payment on the part of the husband is called in Arabic *mahr*, and by English writers *dower*. The latter term is somewhat misleading to those who are only familiar with its narrow signification in modern English law, but, taken in its older and wider sense, is perhaps the least unapt equivalent that our legal vocabulary can supply. Dower, the French *douaire*, the low Latin *doarium*, which again is a corruption of *dotarium*, is evidently a derivative of *dos*, with which indeed it is sometimes used interchangeably; but a more general and more convenient usage employs it to denote a widely different institution, namely, the Teutonic as contrasted with the Græco-Roman type of marriage settlement. Already, near the beginning of the second century A.D., this contrast had begun to attract attention, so that Tacitus noted as a peculiarity of German usage that "the husband brings a *dos* to the wife, instead of the wife bringing it to the husband."* And now, near the close of the nineteenth century, we find the prevailing sentiments of Englishmen and Frenchmen on the subject of matrimony still perceptibly coloured by a corresponding difference, maintained down to quite recent times, in their laws respecting the property of married women.

The sentiment presupposed and encouraged by the dotal system is that matrimony is on the husband's side a burdensome duty, which the wife's family must bribe him to undertake by placing at his disposal, so long as the conjugal union subsists, the income of land or other property which is itself jealously withheld from his control, and which reverts on the termination of the marriage to the wife or to her family.

The sentiment underlying the dower system is that the bride is a prize to be won, if not by the primitive methods of force or purchase from the parents, then by gifts to the maiden herself; which again implies that in the married state the wife is expected to minister to the gratification of the husband, rather than the husband to that of the wife, and that she will have no further opportunity for making acquisitions on her own account. Thus the English dower representing the old German Bride-Price and Morning

* Tacitus, "Germ.," 17.

Gift, consisting originally of whatever the husband chose to declare "at the church door," then limited by law to a certain proportion of his assets, and secured by law up to a certain minimum, was a natural complement and reasonable mitigation of the common law rule of so-called "unity of person," *i.e.*, of the merging of the wife's legal personality in that of the husband.* Ultimately a movement in the reverse direction set in, commencing with the protection of marriage settlements by the Court of Chancery, and culminating in the Married Women's Property Act of 1882, the effect of which has been to make the wife an absolutely distinct person from her husband, able to hold and dispose of property exactly as if she were single, except what may have been placed by means of a marriage settlement under what is practically the dotal system; while side by side with this advance there has been a gradual whittling away of her once considerable and indefeasible rights of inheritance, until the point has been reached that the husband can destroy even her dower-right in a third of his lands and will away from her the whole of his property, real and personal.

The Muhammadan dower resembles the English in being a provision made for the wife out of the property of the husband. It resembles the old, not the modern English dower, in being primarily determined by prenuptial contract, but assessable by a Court of Justice in default of contract, and also in being the consideration for a bargain, of which the chief advantage would otherwise be on the side of the husband. Like the old, but unlike the modern English dower, it has no necessary connection with land, and does, in fact, most often consist of a sum of money. Unlike the English dower of any period, the greater part usually is, and the whole may be, entirely and immediately at the

* This rule, though as old as the Common Law, was of Norman, not of Anglo-Saxon origin. The whole story is admirably told in Kenny's "History of the English Law of Married Women's Property."

disposal of the wife; and even as regards the portion (if any), of which payment has been deferred till the termination of the marriage, though she cannot squander it by anticipation, there is nothing to prevent her releasing it in favour of the husband himself. And, as with the dower, so with all other acquisitions of a married woman, whether made before or after marriage, her power is as absolute and independent as that of an English wife under the Married Women's Property Act, 1882. The doctrine of "unity of person" has no place in Muhammadan matrimonial law. It would, indeed, be intolerable that a woman should lose her proprietary rights, and her freedom of contract, in consequence of a connection which the husband can terminate at his mere caprice at three months' notice.

The Normal Relation Modifiable by Special Stipulation.

This one-sided liberty of divorce, as well as the one-sided permission of polygamy, and the one-sided social restraints imposed on the Moslem wife, are the natural results of complete freedom of contract, and rigid enforcement of contract between parties so unequally matched, as were men and women generally, either in the time of Mahomet or under the Bagdad Caliphate; in the woman's case a life of celibacy impracticable, her chances of acquiring wealth extremely limited, her need of protection extreme; while the man was quite able to live single if he pleased, or to gratify his passions with slave concubines. But where the woman is by any chance in a position to make a better bargain for herself, the same principle of free contract tells in her favour. She, or those negotiating on her behalf, can make it an express term in the marriage contract that the husband shall not take a second wife, or that, if he does, she shall have the option of divorce, or even that he shall divorce her at any time on her demand. And, though an absolute stipulation that she shall never be divorced will be void in law, she can make herself practically secure by stipulating for a dower so large that it will be inconvenient or impossible for him to pay it, on the understanding that it will not be exacted unless he divorces her, or takes a second wife, or otherwise misbehaves. The impossibility of acquiring slave concubines in British India might be expected to strengthen the position of wives in the marriage market; and bargains of this advantageous kind are said to be now not very uncommon.

The Purdah System.

In most Muhammadan communities the legal freedom of women is, to some extent, nullified in practice among the upper classes by the fashion of seclusion, a fashion partly traceable to certain peculiarities of the Muhammadan criminal law, themselves not obscurely connected with personal incidents in the life of the Prophet; partly to a theory of marriage so unsentimental as to encourage but little reliance on personal affection as a substitute for external safeguards of chastity, partly to causes which operate everywhere in proportion to the predominance of the militant over the peaceful elements of society. Before marriage the bride-elect has nothing but gossip to depend on in deciding whether or not to accept the arrangement provisionally made for her by her parents or kinsfolk, with a bridegroom whom she is not supposed even to know by sight. After marriage, her limited opportunities of intercourse with strangers must render it more difficult than in England to bring either law or public opinion to bear against a tyrannical husband, and more easy for him to wheedle or intimidate her into giving up her property, than it would be in England, even without the protection of trustees.

Impunity of Unchaste Wives.

On the other hand, the combination of British-made criminal law and Muhammadan civil law has produced the singular result that in a strictly legal point of view the wife risks absolutely nothing by unchastity. The husband can, no doubt, divorce her for that reason, but he can also divorce her for any other reason, or for no reason. She does not, in any case, forfeit her dower, and the criminal law will have nothing to say to her, but will have much to say to him, should he be provoked to take the law into his own hands. The framers of the Indian Penal Code showed, perhaps, less than their usual regard for logic, when they alleged the harshness of the native laws towards virtuous wives as a reason for according impunity to vicious ones.*

Rules Restrictive of Intermarriage.

Lastly, if we inquire between what persons this somewhat lax and one-sided matrimonial bond may be contracted the answer of Anglo-Muhammadan Law is as follows. The degrees of *consanguinity* which cause prohibition of intermarriage are the same as in England.†

Affinity is only a bar to *successive* unions when it occurs in the direct line of ascent or descent. In other words, a Moslem may marry his *deceased* wife's sister, or his *deceased* brother's widow, though not the widow of his father or of his son. But affinity is a bar to *simultaneous* unions to the same extent as consanguinity. In other words, a Moslem may not have two sisters, nor even an aunt and a niece, in his harem at the same time.

Besides consanguinity and affinity, Muhammadan Law has one ground of prohibition quite peculiar to itself, namely, connection by *fosterage*. A boy and girl suckled by the same woman within an interval of two years become thereby, though otherwise unrelated, no less completely debarred from intermarrying than if they were brother and sister. Such connections were certainly more likely to be known and

* In the Panjab Frontier Districts and Baluchistán a married woman is punishable for adultery. Reg. iv. of 1887, s. 32.

† Short as is the Muhammadan list of prohibitive degrees, that of the Pre-Islamite Arabs was much shorter, allowing, for instance, intermarriage with step-mother and half-sister by the father's side. Some restrictions were expressly imposed by Mahomet (K. iv. 27, Sale, p. 56) and were extended by analogical interpretation.

remembered in ancient Arabia, where the habit was to send the infant to the home of the wet nurse instead of bringing the wet nurse to the child, and to let it remain there sometimes for several years; but why they should be regarded as a bar to intermarriage is a more difficult question, which I must postpone for the present.

Lastly, difference of religion is in some cases a bar to intermarriage. That is to say, it may prevent the union from being recognised as a Muhammadan marriage, leaving its validity to be determined by the law of the non-Muhammadan party. A Moslem woman is considered to have apostatised by marrying a member of any other religious communion; a male Moslem may lawfully marry a Christian or a Jewess, but not an idolatress; consequently, when Akbar and other Mogul Emperors married Rajput princesses the latter were required to make a nominal profession of Islam.*

Parentage.

The Muhammadan system resembles the English, and differs from the Hindú, the Roman, and most of the Rome-derived systems in refusing to recognise adoptive paternity as the source of any legal rights or duties whatsoever. The rights of paternity belong to the lawfully begotten and to no one else. The British Government, having abolished slavery, and with it the possibility of lawfully begetting a child of a female slave and then elevating him to the position of a son by acknowledgment, the only source of legal paternity is conception in lawful wedlock, *proved or legally presumed.* The indulgent English view, that birth after marriage pre-

A very interesting description of Muhammadan domestic life may be read in Mrs. Meer Hassan Ali's "Observations on the Mussulmans of India," published in 1832. The authoress was a Christian, apparently of English parentage, who was married to a Muhammadan of the Shia persuasion, and lived with him for twelve years in Oudh, then a protected native State. "I was received amongst them," she says, "without prejudice, and allowed the free usage of my European habits and religious principles without any attempt to bias or control me."

cludes all question as to the time of conception, is not countenanced by the law of Islam. On the other hand, if a Moslem chooses to acknowledge a boy, who would otherwise be fatherless, as his son, this raises a presumption of legitimacy so strong that our Courts have not quite made up their minds whether any evidence whatever can be admitted to rebut it.

Guardianship.

This branch of Muhammadan Law has been very considerably modified by British legislation, now consolidated in the Guardians and Wards Act, 1890. But some features of the original system still stand out prominently enough to be noticed even in an outline.

In strict law, according to the Hanáfi school, the only kinds of guardianship recognised are (1) that of lunatics, which we need not now consider, and (2) that of minors; though adult women are, if married, subject to certain clearly defined marital rights affecting their personal but not their proprietary independence, and are, if unmarried, dependent on the good offices of male protectors (usually, though not with strict propriety, called guardians) for the chance of accepting or rejecting a husband.

Whether we are concerned with lunatics or with minors, it is convenient to distinguish guardianship of the *person* from guardianship of *property*, and the same individual is not necessarily the fittest for both functions. This distinction is fully recognised by the Indian Guardians and Wards Act, as well as by English and Roman law. But the Muhammadan Law goes further, and distinguishes two kinds of guardianship of the person of a minor, viz. (1) for custody and education (*hizanat*), (2) for contracting in marriage (*jabr*). In respect of the former it is more liberal to the weaker sex than the law of England, in that it gives the custody of young children (boys up to seven, girls to the age of puberty) to the mother as against the father. On the other hand, the disposal in marriage of a girl, and of course *a fortiori* of a boy, is the father's exclusive prerogative, and if he be dead it devolves on the father's father, then on the male agnatic collaterals in order of proximity—even the most remote taking precedence of the mother. The third kind of guardianship, that of property, belongs, of course, primarily to the father; after his death, to the person appointed by his will, if any; in default of a testamentary guardian the appointment rests with the Court, no relative except the father being able to claim the office as of right.

Maintenance.

A very important part of the Law of Family Relations is the regulation of reciprocal rights of maintenance. The Muhammadan Law, like the English, treats property as primarily and naturally individual; it does not, like the Hindú system, contemplate as the normal state of things the existence of a mass of family property, kept together through several generations as a common fund for the common needs, material and spiritual, of its members; nor does it lend itself so easily as English law to artificial imitations of this system by means of entails and family settlements. Only in one case—that of the wife—can a person possessed of property sufficient for his or her maintenance claim to be maintained at the expense of another person. A father is under no obligation to maintain his adult and able-bodied sons, nor his married daughters. Children of either sex who are in easy circumstances must maintain their parents who are poor, whether or not the father is capable of working for his livelihood; but the claims of brothers, uncles and nephews are dependent on the co-existence of all three conditions, poverty and inability to work on their part, and easy circumstances on the part of the relative called upon to maintain them. The claim of poor females depends on their being unmarried, as they are not expected to work for their livelihood. In no case does any liability arise from relationship beyond the prohibited degrees.

Inheritance.

The strongly-marked Individualism of the Muhammadan Law of Family Relations is reflected in their rules of inheritance. There is nothing to suggest or encourage the keeping of a family together after the death of its head; no rule of primogeniture, no theory of universal succession, and, most curious of all, no recognition of the principle of representation. The son of a predeceased son of the proprietor whose inheritance is in question is not considered to stand in the place of his father, and on a level with the surviving sons of his grandfather, as in the Roman, English, and Hindú systems, but is totally excluded by them; * and when son's sons do inherit by reason of no sons having survived, they share all alike as individuals, without reference to the branches to which they belong. And in this, as in other branches of the law, the rights of women are quantitatively inferior to those of men, but similar in kind, and no less clearly defined. The emphatic condemnation by Mahomet of the primitive view that the wives and daughters of a dead man were part of the property to be inherited had for its natural corollary the principle that they should take some definite portion of the inheritance. In accordance with his theory that "men are superior to women," that proportion was fixed at one-half of the share assigned to the corresponding male. Thus, since the husband surviving takes one-fourth of her property, if she leaves issue, one-half if not, the wife surviving her husband takes, in the corresponding cases, an eighth † or a fourth; and son and daugh-

* This happened to be the case with Mahomet himself, so that he owed his start in life entirely to the kindness of one of his uncles. It is the more remarkable that he did not venture to alter a rule, the harshness of which he had himself experienced.

† A wife's share may conceivably be as small as $\frac{1}{32}$, inasmuch as a Moslem is allowed to have as many as four wives, and, in that case, the $\frac{1}{8}$ must be divided amongst them; but, on the other hand the wife has usually something due to her on account of deferred dower, which, like an ordinary debt, takes precedence of all claims of inheritance.

ter, or brother and sister by the same father, divide whatever is not otherwise disposed of in the proportion of two to one. Where, on the other hand, there is a daughter and no son, or a sister and no brother, the female takes half (or two or more together, two-thirds) of whatever is not otherwise disposed of, leaving the rest for the remoter male heirs, whoever they may happen to be. The rule of the "double share to the male" is also applied between the parents, where the case is such (there being no children) that they will inherit together; but as against children the father is only allowed one-sixth, and the mother takes the same, apparently on the ground that a one-twelfth share would be too small to be worth having, or would make the division too complicated. This scheme of apportionment was not expressly prescribed in the Korán in favour of any other females than those above mentioned, and, except by the Shias, has been very sparingly extended by analogy. Females more remote than sisters, as also all males, whose connection with the deceased has to be traced through a female, are relegated to a class called by Arabic writers "heirs of the womb," and, by English writers, "distant kindred," who are postponed to all male agnates, however remote.

Setting aside these, (who, by-the-way, are not admitted at all by the Máliki and Sháfaí schools, and are not thought worthy of the technical appellation of "heirs," even by the Hanáfis), we perceive, that of the heirs properly so-called, some claim a specific fraction of the net assets as being allotted by the Korân to the one or more individuals standing in a particular relation to the deceased, while others simply take whatever is left after the specific fractional claims (if any) have been satisfied. Heirs of the former kind are called, both in English and in Arabic, "sharers;" those of the latter kind are called by English writers, "residuaries," but the Arabic word, so mistranslated, means simply "relatives," as though their title were a natural one, older than the Korán, and merely confirmed by its silence,* whereas that of the Korán would have no existence apart from Scripture.

It will easily be seen that such a system must often involve extremely minute subdivision. In working out the fractions, one of the commonest of common denominators is 24, and denominators of four figures are not unknown. The difficulty of applying such a scheme to landed estates, either large or small, is so manifest, that we might almost have guessed, if we did not know it for a fact, that inheritances did not usually consist of land among the early followers of Mahomet. The Arabs of Mecca had for their principal modes of acquisition trade and plunder, and, for their most valued possessions, slaves and camels, flocks and herds, arms and jewellery; and, during the first period of Saracenic conquest the ordinances of Omar forbade altogether the holding of land by Moslems of the Arab race. When landholding by Moslems became common, as had come to be the case long before the Muhammadan conquest of India, the inconveniences of subdivision were either staved off by simple procrastination, the family occupying the land in common until something occurred to render a partition inevitable, in which case the second generation had to face as best they could the enormously-aggravated perplexities of the arithmetical problem which their predecessors had shirked; or else they were evaded, or mitigated, in certain ways to be presently mentioned.

Lastly, it is interesting to note how the custom of polygamy makes itself felt in the rules regulating the succession of brothers and sisters of the half blood. In monogamous systems, such questions only arise through remarriage of widow or widower, as the case may be. In either case, according to modern English habits, in the latter case only

---

* It is so, in fact, only as regards the males. Daughters with sons, and sisters with brothers, are only brought into the *asabah* by express texts of the Korán.

according to old Roman usage, the first and second families are commonly educated together, so far as difference of age will permit, in one and the same domestic circle and under the same double guardianship. Thus we find on the one hand the old Roman law concerning itself with kinship on the father's side only, placing the consanguine brother on the same level with the full brother and ignoring the uterine brother altogether; and we find on the other hand the English law imitating the latest Roman law in giving no preference at all to the whole blood over the half-blood on either side.

But in polygamous systems, such as the Muhammadan and Hindú, consanguine brothers are more often than not the sons of contemporary wives of the common father; as such they have been brought up in separate establishments, under distinct and not improbably hostile influences, so that, if presumed intimacy and affection be the ground of fraternal succession, there can be no doubt of the priority of the brother by the same father and mother over him who had the same father with the deceased but a different mother. And such is in fact the rule of both systems. As for the uterine brother, that is, the son of the same mother by a different father, the Hindú law cannot contemplate the possibility of his existence, disallowing as it does the re-marriage of widows: the Arabian usage, before Mahomet, ignored him for a different reason, namely that a widow remarrying would leave her children behind her with the family of her first husband, so that they would see little or nothing of her children by the second husband; but a somewhat obscure verse of the Korán was understood to assign to the uterine brother (or sister) a one-sixth share (or one-third to two or more collectively) under the same circumstances as would entitle the full brother and sister to the residue.

Safeguards and Palliatives of the Law of Inheritance.— Wills and Deathbed Gifts.

Tradition ascribes to Mahomet the saying that "the laws of inheritance are one half of useful knowledge," and another tradition makes him responsible for an ordinance which goes far towards justifying the statement by ensuring that the rules of inheritance shall come into operation at the death of every Moslem who has any property to divide. Bequests can only take effect as against legal heirs to the extent of one-third of the property, and by Hanáfi law they cannot take effect at all in favour of one heir to the prejudice of another.* The jurists strove faithfully to check evasions of this severe regulation by regarding a deathbed gift (even if professedly irrevocable) as equivalent to a legacy, and subjecting it to the same restrictions, and by admitting evidence that a sale by a dying man was for inadequate consideration and therefore in part a gift. But they shrank from the impiety of admitting evidence to contradict the acknowledgment of a *debt* by a dying man, thinking it better to leave a loophole for unscrupulous men to cheat their heirs occasionally, than to run the slightest risk of the deceased faring badly at the Day of Judgment through being prevented from paying his just debts.

Wakf, or Endowment.

Another way in which rules of inheritance are in some countries allowed to be evaded is by gifts to a series of persons partly unborn, in other words, by the creation of *entails.* The jurists of Islam might seem to have put an effectual stop to this practice by insisting that the donee

* Hence the remark of the Chief Justice in the Patna case that the alleged transaction was a natural one, because men often leave all their property to their wives, was quite beside the mark. Shahbaz Beg had no power to bequeath to his widow anything additional to her legal fourth. The only possible question was whether he had chosen to dispossess himself of all his property in her favour, while alive and in fair health.

must always be a person in existence and must take actual possession at the time of the gift; but here again they allowed themselves to be disarmed by skilful appeals to pious sentiment. Moslem piety of course encourages endowments for religious purposes, and the lawyers defined religious endowment, in a very liberal and humane spirit, as "the dedication of property in perpetuity to Almighty God in such a way that the income may be used for the benefit of mankind." But are not the endower's own descendants a part of mankind? Why then may he not secure an income in perpetuity for a particular line of them, provided that he completely divests himself of the property while he is alive and in health? The limits within which this evasive device may be employed are differently defined by different ancient authorities, and have been the subject of conflicting decisions in British India.

Pre-emption.

Lastly, the inconveniences resulting from the minute subdivision of land under the rules of inheritance are mitigated in practice, or are at least supposed to be mitigated, by the custom of Pre-emption, according to which, if a person has contracted to sell to a stranger his interest in a piece of land or a house, the benefit of the contract may be claimed, on tender of the price agreed upon, by (1) any one who is joint owner with the vendor of the property in question, or, in default of such, by (2) any one who can show that he is jointly interested in easements connected with the land or house, as (*e.g.*) having a right to use a road passing both properties and not open to the general public, or to irrigate from an adjoining stream, or in the last resort by (3) a mere neighbour. Of course the joint owners here referred to are usually co-heirs of the original acquirer, who chose to go on occupying jointly after his death in order to avoid the worry and inconvenience of the division prescribed by law; and the neighbours are very frequently *quondam* coheirs who have carried out the partition, but whose separate plots of land are so interlaced that life would be intolerable but for various little mutual concessions and arrangements which would be disturbed by the intrusion of a stranger purchaser. But whether on the whole, considering the many openings it gives for misunderstandings and disputes, the rule does more to preserve or to disturb the peace of families, seems to be a matter of dispute among experts. Of the whole number of High Court decisions which are in any way connected with Anglo-Muhammadan Law, not much less than one-third relate to this subject of Pre-emption.

Shia Law.

In order to adapt the above outline to the Shia system the two following almost fundamental differences must be allowed for, besides many others of minor importance.

1. The frankly contractual character of Muhammadan matrimonial law is accentuated still further by the legal recognition of "temporary marriages," that is, not merely terminable at any time by the will of the husband, but which, by the contract, are to terminate automatically at the expiration of a fixed, and sometimes a very short, period, unless renewed by the consent of both parties.*

2. The rules of inheritance make no distinction between the male and female lines of descent, nor, consequently between "residuaries" and "distant kindred."

On the other hand, the principle of representation almost absolutely ignored by the Sunní lawyers, is allowed free scope among claimants in the same degree of proximity to the deceased, though not as between different degrees. Thus a living son will, as by Sunní law, totally exclude the son of a deceased son, and a daughter will take her full Koranic "share" of one-half, instead of the one-third which

---

* See chap. iii. p. 52, and chap. v. p. 79, as to the attempts of Al Mámún and Akbar to overbear the orthodox opposition to these marriages.

would be her portion as a mere co-residuary with the grandson; but if the competition be between daughter's son and son's daughter, (in which case by Sunní law the son's daughter would take one-half as "sharer" and the nearest male agnatic relative the other half), the claimants simply stand in the place of their respective parents, so that the daughter's son will take one-third, and the son's daughter two-thirds.

The whole scheme of succession worked out on these lines certainly wears a more modern aspect than that of the orthodox schools; that is to say, it approximates more nearly to the latest form of the Roman law and therefore to the English Statutes of Distribution and to the Indian Succession Act; but whether Græco-Roman influences had actually anything to do with its development, is mere matter of conjecture.

INDEX.

A

B

C

T

U